Groomed
by a
Gang

I would like to dedicate this book
to my beloved dad, who inspired me to fight back
against the grooming gang and against
the system which failed me and my family.

Groomed
by a
Gang

CHRISTINA O'CONNOR
With *SUNDAY TIMES BESTSELLING*
AUTHOR ANN CUSACK

MIRROR BOOKS

MIRROR BOOKS

All of the events in this story are true,
but some names and details have been changed to
protect the identities of individuals.

1

Published in Great Britain and Ireland in 2023 by
Mirror Books, a Reach PLC business.

www.mirrorbooks.co.uk
@TheMirrorBooks

Print ISBN 9781915306401
eBook ISBN 9781915306418

Printed and bound in Great Britain by
CPI Group (UK) Ltd, Croydon, CR0 4YY

Contents

This book remembers the countless childhoods which have been destroyed by grooming gangs – and also all the children who I hope will be saved in the future.

Prologue

HUDDERSFIELD, JULY 2013

The radio was blaring out the usual golden oldies, and I was just putting the finishing touches to a feathery bob cut when my boss yelled above the music from the other side of the salon.

"We've got a wedding party coming in! Last minute! A dozen up-dos so we need some pins!

"Sounds like we're going to be busy," I smiled.

Opening one drawer after another in the cabinet, I picked out all the hair pins I could find. But at the end of my search, I only had a handful.

"Oh, we need a lot more than that," I groaned.

Up-do hairstyles required lots of pins. And I knew that, back at home, I had stacks. I loved trying out outlandish styles on all of my friends and family, so my bathroom was like a mini salon.

"I'll nip home," I offered. "I can be back in 10 minutes with more pins. I'll bring some clips as well."

Despite being July, it was a grey day, and outside, the cooler air was balm to my hot cheeks.

I was hurrying along, in a purposeful half-jog, when my phone rang. It was a number I didn't recognise and I half-cursed myself for answering. I really didn't have time for this.

"Christina O'Connor?" a voice asked. "Police child safeguarding team here. I wondered if we could have a chat about what happened to you as a teenager?"

I stopped dead in the middle of the pavement. In that moment I was flung back through the years, I was 14 again. Time stood still around me. The traffic skidded to a halt. The entire landscape was frozen. Even my heart seemed to stutter and stop.

You do as you're told, or else…

All thoughts of the hair salon and the up-dos forgotten, I sank to the ground in a crumpled heap, as though my bones had been dissolved in acid. I felt small again, a young teenager again. A frightened, mixed-up child again.

Get out here now or your mum gets it.

Gasping, I gripped the phone, swallowed hard, and tried to find the right words.

"Why now?" I stuttered. "Why? Why are you doing this to me now?"

I was aware my voice was loud, shrill, but I couldn't help it.

Either take this or take a beating. Your choice.

"We are investigating grooming gangs and child sexual exploitation in Huddersfield," she replied. "We'd like to help you."

A strangled sound sneaked out of my throat.

"Help me?" I spat, shocking even myself at the intensity of my bitterness.

"You weren't interested in me then, and you're not interested in me now. If you want to help me, just leave me alone."

I jabbed the red button and slammed my phone back in my pocket. And with my head in my hands, I sobbed. The tears flowed through my fingers, onto my knees, and into a pitiful rivulet down the path. I cried for myself, for what lay ahead. And I cried for the little girl I had once been. For she was lost to me forever.

1

Daddy's Girl

HUDDERSFIELD, AUGUST 2002.

Bouncing excitedly on the bed, I watched as Dad drilled the final part of the bracket onto the wall.

"There you go," he grinned. "All done. You can watch telly in bed tonight, you lucky girl!"

I leapt off the bed and straight into his strong arms; arms that felt to me like they could lift up the whole world.

"Thanks, Daddy," I beamed.

For months, I'd been bending his ear about having a television on the wall in my bedroom. And for months, his answer was always the same:

"It'll ruin the walls! I'm not screwing into perfectly good plaster!"

"Dad, please. Go on!"

"No. And I'm not changing my mind."

"Please!"

But with every refusal, I just smiled to myself, and my resolve grew stronger. I was a daddy's girl, and he and I both knew it. I was confident I could whittle him down, over time.

And on my 11th birthday, in August 2002, there it was: a boxed-up telly, wrapped in shiny pink paper, along with a wall-mounting bracket. My heart's desire.

"Happy birthday, love," he smiled. "You got your own way in the end. You can twist me round your little finger, you know that."

Ours was a happy house; me, my dad, Michael, and my mum, Trish. We had a two-bedroom semi in Huddersfield, West Yorkshire. The house was tiny and my bedroom was just about big enough for a single bed, a wardrobe, and of course the all-important telly on the wall. I had crisp pink Groovy Chick bedding, laundered every weekend without fail by my house-proud mother, and my walls were plastered with posters of *Sabrina, The Teenage Witch* and the *Spice Girls*. If I leaned over the end of the bed, I could stick my head out onto the landing and shout downstairs. There was barely enough room even to get dressed in there. And yet somehow, the lack of space was never an issue. The house was cosy, not cramped. It was welcoming, warm and safe. We were a close family; just like the house, our unit was small but tight-knit. And Dad and I shared an almost tangible bond; a binding thread, spooling through us both, holding us firmly and comfortingly together.

"My girl," he'd say proudly, and it was enough to make my little heart sing.

If he was sitting on the sofa, then I was right there alongside him. If I opened my mouth with a question, he'd often say it first. On Saturdays, for a treat, I'd go out with him in the truck for work. Dad worked as a builder but at weekends he went out 'scotching' or looking for extra jobs. I felt a million dollars sitting up front with him in his white flat back truck, my legs dangling over the end of the rough leather seats. There were oil stains splattered all over the leather and the stuffing had burst through in places. But I loved that truck.

On sunny days, we'd stop off for an ice-cream; the old-fashioned sort, a cold brick of vanilla in between two wafers. That was my Dad all over; old-school and set in his ways. Other days, we'd call in at the chippy; a cone of chips for me, fish and chips for Dad.

"Now, you'd better eat your tea," he'd tell me, in his soft Irish lilt. "Or your mother will have me on toast."

He'd come over from County Kerry early in 1964, just before he turned 17, but never lost his accent. He had Irish colouring too, dark hair and blue eyes, and he was a good 6ft tall and 18 stone. Working outdoors, he had a permanent tan, and a permanent twinkle in his eye.

I liked to think I was a vital member of the Saturday team. I was the right-hand man, passing nails and screws, holding the hammer, clutching onto the ladder for dear life as Dad climbed the rungs one by one. He was more scared of heights than I was, so he'd only ever go up halfway.

"I'm counting on you, pet," he shouted, his voice distant as he cleaned up the brickwork on the front of a house. "Don't let go of that ladder."

My knuckles were white with the effort, my teeth gritted in concentration. Even though he was only about eight feet off the ground, I felt I had his life in my hands and the respon-sibility settled importantly on me. It didn't occur to me then, but Dad of course wanted me to hold the ladder simply so that he knew where I was; it had nothing to do with his own safety, and everything to do with mine.

Some months previously, Mum had enrolled me at Saturday morning dance classes, but I screwed up my face at the leotard and the pumps. It just wasn't my thing at all. More than anything, I regretted that they had replaced my Saturday morning trips with Dad. I missed those. I missed the chips and the ice-cream and the radio blaring out the football news. I missed passing the hammer, counting the nails. I missed being absolutely invaluable. So, after a few pointless lessons in jazz and tap, I was back in the van in my old jeans and my duffle coat. Where I belonged.

Late in the afternoon, after a hard day holding the ladder, Dad would take me to the Irish Centre or to St Patrick's social club.

"A swift one before teatime," he'd say with a wink. "Better not keep your mother waiting."

Creatures of habit, we both had the same order every time; mine was a red Lucozade and a packet of cheese and onion crisps, Dad's was a pint of Guinness. He'd make me look away for a second, pointing out an imaginary spider as a distraction, before nicking a drop of Lucozade for his drink. Of course I always knew the trick was coming, and I always played along. I loved to see the small red spot of Lucozade bleeding out into the white froth of the Guinness.

Back at home, Mum would have a big evening meal ready, a stew or a bolognese, or Dad's favourite: bacon, mash, cabbage and turnip. She was a chef by trade and her cooking was top-notch. Physically, and also in personality, I was more like my mother. She was around 5ft 3 ins with fair hair, dark eyes and a friendly face. She had a quick temper too, which was easily calmed, just like me, and we often bickered and clashed. Dad was laid-back and soft-hearted, a sociable man who could hold a conversation with anyone, but considered each word carefully before it left his mouth.

"Oh, but you've kissed the Blarney Stone," he'd tell me – referring to a tradition that is said to give a person the gift of eloquence – as I chatted away all morning in the truck. "Don't you ever pause for breath?"

He and Mum had first met at a wedding, where she was bridesmaid, and he was best-man. Mum was just a teenager at the time but loved to tell the story of how she had fallen for him that same day. A few years later, they started dating, and had been very much in love ever since. Though they were completely different, they complemented each other perfectly. I used to love listening to the well-worn tale of their romance, over and over again.

"You'll fall in love too one day," Dad told me with a smile. "When the time is right."

On weekdays, after the washing up was done, Mum and I liked to binge on the soaps back to back; *Emmerdale*, *Coronation Street*, *EastEnders*. Dad watched the news every night, and nothing else. But at weekends, he and I would curl up on the couch and watch reruns of *Father Ted*, *Only Fools and Horses* and *Steptoe and Son*. At first, I didn't even understand half of the jokes. I only laughed because Dad was laughing. But that was more than good enough for me.

* * * *

With Dad's Irish roots, St Patrick's Day was practically a state occasion in our house. Mum had Irish grandparents too, and a rich seam of Gaelic heritage ran through us all. For weeks before the day itself, we'd make pom-poms for the parade, and help to sell the programmes.

"What about this?" I asked Mum, showing her my latest design for a St Patrick's Day poster. "I'm going to need more green felt-pen."

As part of the celebrations, Irish bands and singers would come over to perform at the Irish Centre and so we'd get involved with the catering and the preparations. For me, as a kid, it was like a second Christmas. I loved baking soda bread with Mum, singing the old Irish songs with Dad and proudly pinning a shamrock onto my coat when we went out. Dad had taught me the lyrics to all of his favourite songs:

"But for all that I found there I might as well be, in the place where the dark Mourne sweeps down to the sea…"

Though we were not devoutly religious, I'd attended a Roman Catholic primary school. When it was time to study our Sacramental Programme, Dad ferried me and all my friends to the weekly lessons at the local church, in his truck. It was like a day out, all piling in together, clutching our Bibles and our rosary beads. Dad seemed to bring the fun into every occasion, even our stuffy lessons with the local priest.

Dad was originally from Brosna, a village to the north-east of Kerry, a landscape of craggy mountains and peat bogs, a place where the rain from the hills and the mist from the fields met in the middle to form a permanent haze. But for me, having listened carefully to all the lessons at church, I knew it was the closest I would ever get to Heaven on Earth.

Every summer, we'd spend three weeks holidaying in Brosna with Dad's extended family. They were great times with my Irish cousins; trips to the coast and days out at the annual Puck Fair and the local festivals. It rained more often than not, but somehow that just added to the whole appeal. We learned to be ludicrously grateful even for a moderately dry day. And at the first sign of the sun, we'd cram into the car with raucous excitement, carrying buckets and spades and crab lines.

"The beach! The beach!"

One year, there was an unexpected heatwave and Dad fell asleep at the beach. He normally tanned so easily but the sun was especially hot and he woke up glowing red raw with sunburn. He had white circles around his eyes where his sunglasses had been, and white stripes on his feet from his flip-flops.

"You look like a stripy deckchair!" we laughed. "Come on, let's get you inside."

The great thing about Ireland was that the hot weather never lasted, and Dad was grateful for the torrential rain the next day. Coming home to Huddersfield was always sad, because we were leaving all the noise and the chaos and the warmth behind. And it wasn't the warmth of the weather that I missed the most. There was no welcome like an Irish one, and I felt such a bond with my cousins that it hurt me to say goodbye.

On her days off, in the school holidays, Mum took me for trips out to Scarborough and Blackpool too. We made many happy memories on the beach, riding the donkeys, screaming on the roller-coasters, dropping our sandwiches in the sand. But County Kerry would always have a special place in my heart.

And that summer of 2002, with my new TV on the wall, I spent many an hour tucked up in my Groovy Chick bed, watching reruns of *Father Ted* or the *EastEnders* omnibus, with my grey and white cat, named Vicky, who we'd inherited from my grandmother when I was small. I didn't realise it, but those times were golden. Innocent, precious, and tragically temporary. And all too soon, to be snatched away.

2

'Oi, Fatty!'

I started at high school in September 2002. My uniform; a pink and white checked shirt, a navy blue jumper, navy blue trousers, had been hanging on the back of the living room door for days. It was not as daunting as it might have been, as most of the kids from my primary school were moving up with me, so there was an element of security and reassurance alongside the apprehension. Whatever lay ahead, we were in it together. That first morning, Mum and Dad had arranged to go into work a little later so that they could wave me off. Dad took my photo in the hallway, with my new backpack on and my jumper sleeves hanging over the ends of my fingers.

"I can't believe it," he said, his eyes shiny with tears. "My little girl, off to high school."

They'd bought me a new mobile phone, my first ever, so that they knew I was safe each day. But I was so thrilled with the novelty, I'd already used up most of the credit that first morning by calling and texting my mates from my bedroom! I got on the bus with one of my cousins and some of our friends from primary school. My new high school, again Roman Catholic, was two bus rides and around 20-minutes away from my home, but it felt increasingly as though we were crossing a border as we huffed slowly through the rush hour. I had never felt so far from the familiarity of home as I stepped off the second bus and into the grey drizzle of the school yard, picking my way through throngs of kids, all taller than me, all seemingly knowing where they were going, all imbued with that inner self-confidence I craved. As I walked, I picked up on snippets of conversation and scattered giggles and hoped that soon I would be included in one of these bubbles of friendship. But I hadn't even made it across the tarmac when a voice from the crowd shouted:

"Oi, Fatty!"

The words stung like a slap. Instantly, I tried to shrink into my new winter coat, wishing myself into invisibility. I didn't dare turn around, let alone retaliate.

"Just ignore him," muttered my friend, Leanne.

But again, as we lined up for our form rooms, another voice quipped:

"Look at Miss Piggy over there. She's been on the pies all summer!"

A collective snigger rippled through the whole queue, and I felt my cheeks burn with shame. It was true, I carried a few extra pounds. I wasn't fat, necessarily, but I'd always been a chubby child, with a round face. Most of my family was a little overweight and it was just accepted that that was the way we were.

"You're not fat, you're big boned," Mum would always tell me, with a reassuring smile.

It had never been a big deal. Until now. But I was fast

learning that high school was a harsh and unforgiving landscape and even a few pounds extra would not, under any circumstances, go unnoticed or unchecked. As the days went by, the taunts and the jibes became a regular part of my day. And though I shrugged the bullies off with what I hoped was an indifferent stare, deep down, the words really hurt.

"How was your day, love?" Mum would ask, as I dumped my bag in the hallway and went upstairs to change out of my uniform. Mum was a stickler for that; if my school uniform wasn't hung up immediately after I got home, she'd have something to say about it.

"Fine," I mumbled.

I knew, if she got even a whiff of how miserable I was, she'd insist on speaking to my teachers, and that would just make the bullies even worse. I had to cope with this on my own. And my way of coping, frustratingly, perversely, was simply to eat more. Mum cooked healthy and wholesome meals at home. But Dad was a soft touch, and I could usually scrounge a fiver off him, before he left for work.

"Make it last all week," he'd tell me.

But inevitably it was gone that same day, on soothing sweets, crisps and fizzy drinks. The food was both a comfort and a curse. I resented those calories, and yet I craved them too. Each Haribo, each square of Dairy Milk, helped to ease the ache inside me. But it was short-lived, of course, for every sugar rush was inevitably followed by a crushing, devastating low. And the next morning, in the school yard, it was back to the same old routine.

"Hey! Miss Piggy!"

Faced with the constant jibes, the name-calling, the cruel jokes, the sniggering, I crumbled, bit by bit, day by day.

"What're you troughing today?"

"You! Blob! Don't come near me, you might eat me!"

Sometimes, in the canteen queue, I'd feel a sharp prod in the back, followed by:

"Just checking if you're cooked yet, Miss Piggy."

Then, when I sat down on a plastic chair in the dining room, there'd be an over-dramatic intake of breath, as if they all expected my chair to snap and give way. As the tears stung my eyes, my tray would be swiped dramatically onto the floor, my dinner splattered all over the tiles like a culinary car crash.

"Never mind! We all know you don't need the calories, Fatty!"

I was utterly miserable. I was not really confident enough to stand up for myself, especially not in a new school, and certainly not against a wall of solid hostility. It was draining and exhausting, and as the months dragged by, I felt whittled away, eroded, like a sandcastle in the rain. It didn't help either that I wasn't an academic child, I didn't enjoy my lessons and I often struggled to follow the teacher's train of thought. For most of the kids, the PE lesson was a welcome escape from the tedium of trigonometry or romantic poetry. But it was hell for me. I felt as though I was laid bare, hung out to dry, as I shuffled out of the changing rooms, in my PE kit, my legs already mottled with cold.

Year Seven finished, and there was a temporary reprieve during the summer holidays with the highlight of those glorious, uncomplicated weeks spent in County Kerry. But all too soon, I was out with Mum, shopping for a new uniform, standing awkwardly in the changing rooms. And at a size 14 I was two sizes bigger than most of my pals.

"Can I get some new baggy clothes as well?" I asked her.

I just wanted to wear loose sweatshirts and joggers all through the summer. I wanted to hide away. And then, with none of the anticipation of the previous September, it was time to start Year Eight. That first morning back, the bullies picked up right where they had left off.

"Hey, Fatty! Are you in plus size trousers or what?"

I'd harboured a foolish glimmer of hope that perhaps they might forget about me over the holidays and find someone else to pick apart. But of course, I was wrong. And after a break, coming back to the abuse was all the more painful. The words wounded me more than ever. Every day I was on high alert, waiting for the next attack, the next jibe, and it was as inevitable and depressing as the homework I struggled with each night. It was so lonely, too. I felt as though nobody understood how sad and desperate I was feeling. My school day had become utterly intolerable. And so, I took the only way out I could see.

* * * *

There was no feeling quite like it; tearing across the muddy school field, my ponytail streaming in the wind, my bag slapping against my arm as I ran.

"Quick Tina!" yelled my friend, Macie. "I can see Miss Williams at the window!"

'Oi, Fatty!'

I knew from bitter experience that it was hard to run and laugh at the same time, but I couldn't help myself. The thought of our deputy head dashing across the field after us, her high heels sinking into the sludge, was terrifying and hilarious in equal measure. I dissolved into giggles, my legs suddenly slow and jelly-like underneath me.

"Stop!" I gasped breathlessly, flapping my arms. "I need a minute!"

Bending double as a wheeze caught in my throat, I hitched my bag back onto my shoulder. But then Macie shouted:

"Shit! She's coming after us! She's climbing the gate in her pleated skirt! Look!"

A wave of panic surged through me and, resisting the temptation to look back and see our deputy-head wedged on the gate, I set off again, faster this time, towards the bottom of the field. When we reached the fence, I threw myself over it like an unwanted parcel and landed in a crumpled heap on the other side. The contents of my bag spilled out onto the verge and, red-faced and panting, I gathered up my books, my favourite glittery ruler, and a couple of leaky pens. Now, the alley was only a few steps away. Salvation was in sight.

"Made it!" I grinned, as Macie and I both skidded around the corner and into the alleyway together. "I wonder if she's still stuck on the gate?"

We laughed together as we made our way down onto the main road, away from school, away from the bullies. For 13 years, I had been a model daughter, and then a model student. I had never stepped out of line. Until now, I hadn't had a single unauthorised absence or a detention, or even a late mark on my school record. But now, faced with the misery and the predictability of the school bullies, I had started to play truant.

Each morning after registration, me and a couple of pals from the years above me at school would walk calmly past the deputy head's office and out of the building, before dashing across the fields opposite and away to safety. We were clearly visible from the office window as we made our escape, but in many ways, the flaws in our plan made it so much more exciting. I was fast discovering that skipping school was exhilarating, and it was fun; the sense of adventure all the sweeter because we knew we were breaking every rule.

* * * *

The good thing, and also the bad thing, about truancy was that it was addictive. That first time we ran out of school, it had seemed so ridiculously naughty, so rebelliously bad, that I was convinced it would all end in tears. I certainly didn't plan to do it more than once. It wasn't even my idea; I simply followed one of my friends who was so much braver than I was. All that afternoon, as we hung around the park, and I spent my £5 on cheese and onion crisps and a family size bar of chocolate, I expected to see our deputy head, looming over a hedge or jumping out from behind the swings. But there was nothing and nobody to catch us out.

"We got away with it," Macie smiled.

That night, I went home at the usual time, and Mum said: "How was school?"

"Yeah, good," I replied, incredulously.

Clearly, she had no idea either. And the next morning, as I went into class for registration, nobody gave me a second glance. I was both relieved, and a little aggrieved. How could they not have noticed we had missed a whole day off school? Was I so easily dispensed with? It felt wrong that skipping school was so straightforward.

"It's so easy," Macie said under her breath. "Let's do it again. Get your mark and we'll scarper."

And so, it became a routine. For weeks, we went into school, we registered, and then, bold as brass, we simply left. We walked sedately down the corridor, mingling in with the crowd, but the minute we reached the main doors, we tore out of the school and across the field. We knew we could be seen from the office; we knew a teacher might run after us. We felt like bandits, on the run, whooping as we raced through the wet grass. As far as we were concerned, we were outlaws on the margins of society. I was 13 years old, and I was living on the edge.

3

New Friends

It started off as a completely normal morning, in September 2005. I had just turned 14 a few days before, celebrating with a trip to see a Harry Potter film at the cinema with Mum and my cousins. And now we were into another school year. But already, in the first week, the gloss had worn off the new term and I was idly toying with the idea of truanting, yet again.

Together with a couple of pals, I got the 356, as usual, to the bus station, at around 7.45am. Inside the station, we met up with a gaggle of our classmates, some squeezed onto benches, others already queueing for the 64 which would take us to the school gates. We joined the queue, impatiently fidgeting, complaining and shivering. The weather was cold and damp, the sky hanging low and streaked with dark purples and greys. And though we were under the shelter of the bus station, it was draughty and bleak. I huddled against a concrete pillar and thought longingly of my Groovy Chick duvet, wishing I was back in bed. Even with the promise of escaping lessons after registration, I had no enthusiasm for the day ahead. I was still shivering on the edge of the queue with a couple of my friends, Macie and Lara, when three young men, all much older than us, came sauntering over.

"What are your names?" asked the tallest one. He had a wispy goatee beard and was clearly the leader of the group; confident and self-assured, bordering on being a bit confrontational. He was wearing a tracksuit with brown Rockport boots, which were immaculately clean. I remember thinking they were probably brand-new, and I was envious. I knew those boots weren't cheap.

"I'm Christina," I said. "Tina."

Mum hated me shortening my name, but I was in one of those moods.

"Pretos," he replied, handing me a cigarette. "Smoke?"

I didn't want to admit, in front of him and his pals, that I was just 14 years old and hadn't had a cigarette before.

"Yeah," I said, hoping I sounded indifferent and unimpressed.

The other two introduced themselves as Glen and Manny. Pretos told us he worked as a mechanic. At 22, he was eight years older than me. The other two looked a year or two younger than him, Glen was skinny and Manny was quite short with a cute face. They were all British Asians of Pakistani heritage. We had school uniforms on, so there was no point in us telling lies about our ages. We were quite obviously children. I choked a little on the cigarette before passing it to one of my friends. And just as our bus arrived, she exchanged numbers with Pretos.

"We're meeting them in the park tonight, after school," she

told me excitedly as we climbed onto the bus. "Told me he's bringing a surprise! You coming or what?"

My eyes were still watering from the cigarette, but there was no way I was going to miss out on the fun.

"Just try and stop me," I smiled.

Later that afternoon, perfectly timed with the arrival of the bus, I dashed home to change my uniform, looking for all the world as though I had been at school all day, before racing out again moments later.

"Going to Macie's!" I shouted to Mum. "Won't be long."

"In before dark," she reminded me. "Be careful, love."

The park, or 'the rec' as we called it, was only a two minute walk from my house and by the time I arrived, my friend, Macie, and another pal, Caroline, were waiting on the swings. I didn't really think that Pretos and his mates would show up but sure enough, quite soon after, a black Micra screeched to a halt on the road opposite and they all got out.

Pretos was driving and he was the one holding a carrier bag, with the tell-tale clink of bottles inside, as he walked towards us.

"Hey girls," he grinned. "Brought you a little something, just like I promised."

He produced a bottle of vodka, a bottle of Bacardi, and a packet of Benson and Hedges. I gave Macie a sideways look as he unscrewed the vodka and handed it to me.

"Here," he said. "You get started, gorgeous."

I giggled. I'd never had vodka in my life before. The nearest I got to alcohol was when Dad let me have a small sip of his Guinness with my Red Lucozade mixed in the froth. Like most 14-year-olds, I'd certainly never been drunk. We passed the vodka around, and though I took tiny sips it burned the back of my throat, smarting right up to my nose and eyes. I could barely see straight.

"That's nice," I gasped, choking a little, and Pretos laughed indulgently.

I took another sip, and it tasted better this time, less toxic. I was torn between letting myself go completely and fretting about facing my parents later. They would surely smell the alcohol on me. The cigarette smoke was easier to explain away; Mum and Dad were both social smokers, so it wasn't unusual to have a passing whiff of smoke in the hallway, especially on a coat or a jacket. But I knew there was no way I could go home drunk. Much as I wanted to impress our new mates, and I was getting a taste for the vodka too, my overriding feelings were of doubt and trepidation. As dusk fell, I felt a mix of frustration and relief.

"Time for me to go," I said sheepishly. "Got to be in at home."

I expected them to snigger, but instead the men nodded and said their goodbyes, and Pretos slipped me an extra-strong mint.

"Get rid of the booze smell on your breath," he explained. "You don't want any trouble."

Me and my friends left at the same time and, as we reached the gate, Pretos shouted:

"Same time, same place tomorrow, yeah?"

We all burst into helpless giggles, frothed up no doubt by the vodka on an empty stomach.

"Yeah sure!" I replied.

When I looked back, at the top of the road, the three men had faded into the encroaching darkness and were no more than fuzzy, uncertain outlines against the backdrop of the children's slide and swings. It had been such a strange evening. And now, as they dissolved like phantoms into the night air, it was as though it had never happened at all.

* * * *

Mum had an Irish stew waiting when I got home, which was the perfect antidote to the alcohol. Sitting down and eating, soaking up the vodka, the giddy feeling quickly evaporated.

"How was Macie?" Mum asked. "Did you have a nice time?"

"Yeah, good," I replied neutrally.

"And what about school?" she pressed. "Did it go okay?"

"Yeah, good."

I didn't mention, of course, that I had played truant for the entire day. And I definitely didn't mention that I had been on the rec with three young men who were several years older than I was.

Paddock, our area of Huddersfield, was like a macrocosm of our family; close-knit with a strong sense of belonging. I was proud to be a member of the Irish community, and my family's social life revolved mainly around the Irish Centre and around Mum's relatives who lived nearby. There were no official rules, and there was no segregation as such. But it was accepted and tacitly encouraged that we stayed within our own locality. *Stick with what you know.* That was the message. So to meet strangers, and men from a different area and a different background, was out of bounds for so many reasons. Mum and Dad, I knew instinctively, would not have approved of my new friends. I was right of course, but for completely the wrong reasons. Naïve, innocent and foolish in the way that only know-all teenagers can be, I thought my parents' main concern would be the vodka and the Bacardi. I had no idea how sinister and disturbing my new friendships really were. And because I thought, at 14, that I was worldly and streetwise, that I could look after myself, I would have to learn the hard way. The hardest way imaginable.

'U drunk?' I texted Macie, before I went to bed. 'I luv vodka! My new fave!'

'Me 2' she replied. 'Feel a bit sick tho.'

The following afternoon, after school had finished, I couldn't wait to get to the park again. This time, we spotted the black Micra as it turned the corner. Pretos was driving, naturally. He seemed to be in charge of everything.

Today was brighter, and warmer too, and the streets were busier. There were some children in the park, and dog walkers on the paths behind. I felt a stab of worry that I might bump into a neighbour or a family friend, who would definitely report back to my parents. Girls like me just didn't hang around the park with older men. I knew definitely that it was wrong, but I didn't really know why.

"Keep an eye out," Macie muttered under her breath. "We're bound to get grassed up sooner or later."

Even though it was warm, she pulled her hood up, over

her face, and I did the same. But, as the vodka was passed back and forth, my worries seemed to fragment and float away into the clear afternoon skies. I couldn't deny, there was an edge to misbehaving that I really liked. Knowing I was being deliberately and blatantly defiant, knowing my behaviour was strictly forbidden, just made it all the more appealing. Playing truant from school and arranging clandestine meetings with strangers seemed to go hand in hand. It was a new phase of my life; a growing up, a coming of age, I told myself.

"Come on, swig off the rest of the vodka," Pretos said. "I'll take you out for a ride."

I stared at him, at once wary and excited.

"What? In your car?" I asked.

"Yeah," he laughed. "What else? Get in!"

I wasn't allowed out of our locality. Mum and Dad had very clear rules and my boundary was the park itself. But I didn't want to miss out on the fun either. The worst thing I had done in my life, so far, was to once scrawl my name in very small letters on the underside of the children's slide in the park. Now, I was getting into a strange car, with a strange man, with a bottle of vodka in my hand. I didn't know whether I was supremely lucky or supremely stupid. But, as I took another gulp, I realised I didn't really care which it was. We crammed six people into the tiny Micra and I felt a guilty pang about travelling without a seat belt, as if that should be my greatest concern.

"Keep your heads down," I said to Macie and Caroline. "Hoods up."

Pretos drove us first to a local snooker hall, where we went inside and waited, shyly, whilst he spoke with a group of middle-aged men in the far corner. There was a thick smog of dust and cigarette smoke, which hovered in oblong patches below the low lights which hung over the tables. It was mysterious, sinister almost, and I felt a sort of anxious thrill. I was totally out of my depth, yet I didn't want to turn back. The men waved and smiled encouragingly in our direction, and I smiled back politely. On our way out, I nipped into the toilets, which were grubby and stank of a putrid mix of cannabis and urine.

"They liked you," Pretos said, as we walked back outside, and I gulped at the fresh air.

I should have been appalled by the whole experience, but my teenage self couldn't help but feel flattered and impressed.

"I liked them too," I said, remembering my manners.

This was all new to me. It was a lifestyle I'd never glimpsed before and I wanted to see more. We got back in the car and passed the vodka around again.

"Duck down," Pretos ordered, as he revved the engine. "Don't want your mum spotting you, do we?"

We did as he instructed and again, instead of alarm bells ringing, I just thought he was being thoughtful, trying to keep us out of trouble. Pretos drove us around the streets and then down towards the canal, stopping briefly at a taxi firm there. We had bassline music blaring and the windows down. Pretos was smoking, with his elbow resting on the open window. Once or twice, he took his hands off the steering wheel and closed his eyes.

"Can't see a thing!" he yelled, knocking back a couple of pills from out of his pocket. "Be afraid, girls! Very afraid!"

I should have been petrified. The alarm bells should have been screaming in my ear by now. Instead, I felt a growing sense of awe and excitement. I felt so grown up, so much older and wiser than I had been just a few days before. We badgered Pretos to play some Britney Spears and we sang along to the music, sharing the Bacardi, passing round cigarettes and sweets. Next, Pretos parked up at the cinema and began flicking through the film times on his phone.

"I can't stay to watch a film," I said anxiously. "I need to go home soon. My mum will be on my case."

"Yeah," Macie nodded. "Me as well."

Instead Pretos bought chips and kebabs from a nearby takeaway, and we ate in the car before he screeched off again, hands in the air as he drove, sparking more peals of laughter from the back seat.

"We'll crash!" I yelled, more agog than afraid.

More than anything, I felt a sense of belonging and togetherness that I'd never had at school. Pretos and the others never mentioned my size. They didn't even seem to notice that I was overweight.

I'd finally found friends – real friends – who liked me and accepted me just the way I was. Exhilarated, pumped up with adrenalin and booze, I sang louder and louder.

'Baby can't you see I'm calling?

'A guy like you should wear a warning…'

But when Pretos turned into the road to the park, and I saw my house in the distance, the words suddenly dried and withered in my throat. Sliding down the back seat, so that I was completely hidden in the footwell, I hurriedly passed the Bacardi bottle to Glen.

"Feel a bit sick," I mumbled.

I felt a jab of guilty shame when I imagined Mum peering out of the window, wondering where I was. But it was quickly smothered by a ripple of excitement as Pretos turned up the music and winked at me over his shoulder.

"Live a little, eh?" he yelled above the thumping bass. "Don't worry, I'll drop you at the end of the street. They won't know where you've been. Stop stressing."

He was right. I was a teenager. I was *supposed* to push the boundaries and outrage the older generation. This was exactly what being young was all about.

* * * *

For the rest of the week, I didn't see the gang again. I had a dentist's appointment one afternoon, and so Mum collected me from the school gates. And then the next day, we were invited out for tea to my grandparents.

'Where r u?' Pretos texted. 'Missin' u!'

I was missing the men too, or, more specifically, the sense of adventure and rebellion that they brought hurtling along with them. Now my little bedroom, with the TV on the wall, which had once seemed so cosy and safe, seemed poky and stifling. I felt hemmed in. As though I was missing out on life. As though I was being held back and slowed down, and all the fun was happening elsewhere. Normally, I enjoyed visiting my grandparents with Mum and Dad, but now, I resented it as terminally boring.

"Why do I have to come for tea with you two?" I grumbled. "I'm a teenager. I'm not a kid. I've got my own plans, you know."

That weekend, I made an excuse that I was nipping out to see Macie, and I arranged with Pretos to meet up at the park. I was usually a bit of a tomboy, happy in old jeans and joggers, but I'd made a special effort today. I was wearing my favourite green and yellow Kerry football shirt, a gift from Dad, and even a bit of make-up.

"Have you got mascara on?" Mum asked suspiciously as I sidled past her in the hall.

I blushed, caught out, hoping she wouldn't send me back upstairs to wash it off. She and Dad were strict about make-up, they both thought I was too young.

"Well," she sighed. "I suppose mascara won't hurt. Only at weekends though, mind?"

I smiled and skipped out of the door and down to the park. Today, Pretos was already waiting, and herded us quickly into the Micra. Glen squashed in next to me and, as we drove off, sandwiched together in the back, I felt his hand searching for mine. I held my breath, not daring to make eye contact, but not snatching my hand back either. I'd never had a boyfriend before; this was the first time. I'd never even held hands with a boy my own age, never mind a man. I didn't stop to question whether I wanted to be his girlfriend, or whether I wanted him to hold my hand. The idea of being in a relationship mattered more to me, at 14, than the person I was with. And the fact that Glen was several years older didn't concern me at all; if anything, it gave the relationship validity and kudos. This was yet more proof that I was growing up, growing away from my parents and finding my own way in the world.

Close up, Glen stank of stale smoke and his breath was sour from vodka. But I ignored it, telling myself this was how men really smelled. Glen ran his fingers down my cheek, pulling the bobble out of my ponytail and looping my hair instead behind my ears.

"I prefer it like this," he said.

I preferred my ponytail, but I said nothing. I was on a natural high, I couldn't believe I had my very own boyfriend, I couldn't wait to tell everyone at school tomorrow. Not only did I have a boyfriend, but he was older, and he bought me vodka, cigarettes and takeaways. This would give the bullies something to think about. I felt like this was my payback time. Something good was happening to me, at last. As we reached the junction of the next road, Pretos unexpectedly took a turn up towards the reservoir.

"Where are we going?" I asked, panicking. I wasn't allowed up this road, and the reservoir was a couple of miles away. It was way outside of my boundaries and my comfort zone.

"We're going for a drink and a smoke. Just relax," he said.

I thought I could sense an edge in his voice, so I said nothing else. But when we arrived at the reservoir, my heart sank. There were people around, walking and cycling. There was bound to be someone here who recognised me. I didn't even want to get out of the car. I was worried too about getting home on time before dark. But Pretos was clearly in no hurry. He switched off the engine, changed the music, and began expertly rolling what I realised was a joint between his fingers. Once again, I was caught squarely between rules and rebellion. I'd never tried drugs before. Part of me couldn't wait, part of me was dreading it. Pretos lit the joint and passed it around, but I made my excuses and stared miserably out of the window as the light faded. Then, almost drowned out by the music, my phone rang in my pocket. I knew, without checking, it would be my mum.

"It's her mum," Glen said urgently, glancing at my phone. "Switch the music off."

"Yeah, be quiet," Pretos hissed.

I answered nervously, and she said:

"Your tea is ready. I've done gammon with mash. Are you on your way home?"

"Yep," I replied casually. "Won't be long. I am on the bus back from Macie's. It's round the corner now." Macie lived a few miles away, so it was easy for me to argue I was late because of the buses. They never ran on time.

I hung up and we all laughed loudly at the lie. The bubble of tension which had been building was so easily popped.

"Guess that means we need to get you back," Pretos smiled, starting the engine.

I was so relieved that I'd got away with it. Grateful too, to my new mates for covering for me. I was fast learning that I could rely on these men. They had my back in a way that people my own age, at school, just didn't understand. We raced back into Paddock and I scurried in through the front door, just as Mum and Dad were sitting down at the dining table.

"You took your time!" Mum said. "We've been waiting."

I said little during the meal and afterwards vanished upstairs to my bedroom. I was in my pyjamas, glued to my telly, when Mum marched in, her eyes blazing.

"So, you were at Macie's all afternoon?" she asked, her voice shaking with anger.

I felt my blood run cold. This was exactly what I had been anticipating.

"Yeah," I said insolently.

"Well, that's funny," she snapped. "Because you were spotted in a car with a load of Asian blokes at 4.30pm. How do you explain that?"

She was shouting now, one hand on her hip, the other waving madly in my direction.

I shrugged. I could see no other way except a flat denial.

"Well?" she yelled, her voice sharp and furious. "Who are they? What the hell have you been up to?"

I shrugged again.

"No idea what you're on about," I said sulkily. "Told you, I was at Macie's. Ask her. I don't know any Asian men and I haven't been in a car."

Mum snorted.

"There's something going on," she said. "I can tell. I know when you're lying. You're grounded all week. You come straight home from school, and you don't go out. Understand?"

Now it was my turn to shout.

"A whole week? Really?"

The problem was, Mum and I were so similar. We both had hot tempers, short fuses. We clashed terribly in arguments; two fireworks, hissing and spitting at each other. Dad, completely different, was calm and composed. He rarely raised his voice. After Mum had slammed down the stairs, he came and popped his head round my bedroom door.

"I hope you're behaving yourself," he said, each word carefully considered and weighed before it left his mouth. "I would be disappointed if you let us down, pet."

The words were like a knife through me. I couldn't bear the thought of letting him down. His quiet words hit harder than any punishment or reprimand from my mother.

"Honestly, Dad, I'm telling the truth," I said. "She's got me mixed up with someone. I wasn't in anyone's car. I've been with Macie the whole time."

But I couldn't meet his eyes, and I felt his gaze, burning into the side of my head, right through to my soul. He knew I was lying.

"You know how much we love you," he said, and then he closed the door.

* * * *

That weekend, Mum and Dad kept a close eye on me. We went to the Irish Centre on Friday night and again on Sunday afternoon, meeting up with my grandparents and other relatives. Mum had baked soda bread to wrap in warm tea towels and hand out to family members, and normally I enjoyed helping her. I especially liked kneading the dough; throwing it around the work surface until it was springy and elastic. But this time, I just couldn't be bothered. Baking bread seemed so boring, so suburban and childish. I pictured Pretos and the others screeching around the streets in the Micra, knocking back vodka and smoking weed. I thought of Glen and panicked that perhaps he'd find a new girlfriend whilst I was grounded.

"Please let me out, Mum," I begged. "Please. I need to see my mates. You don't understand."

Mum pursed her lips and shook her head.

"You need to do as you're told, young lady," she retorted.

By Sunday night, I was desperate. I went to my room and played my Britney Spears music full blast and ignored Mum yelling at me in protest from the bottom of the stairs.

"Turn it down!" she shouted, thundering into my room.

"Let me go out!" I yelled. "You won't have to listen to it then!"

It was a war of attrition. I made myself as difficult and noisy and awkward as possible, hoping they would cave in. And, four days in, they'd had enough.

"We've decided you can go to Macie's," Mum said. "Just this once. But I want to speak to Macie, and to her mother, to make sure you're there."

Inwardly, I was whooping, but I nodded seriously. I knew Macie's mother worked late, so I just needed Macie to send a text on her behalf. By the next afternoon, I was free again. And it was great, being part of the gang again, hanging around the park, sharing a first kiss with Glen, writing our names inside a love heart in the condensation on the slide. I was so relieved just to be out of the house and away from the scrutiny and criticism of my parents. And when the vodka and the spliffs were passed around, I accepted without a second thought. This was all my mother's fault, I told myself. She had driven me to this, pushing me away from my family, and towards the gang. She treated me like a kid, and I deserved better. I wanted a break from her, a break from the rules. I needed a chance to grow up and be myself.

Even so, when Pretos produced his car keys, I felt a prickle of unease.

"Sit in," he smiled. "I promise I won't drive off with you! I won't go to the reservoir."

There was a glint in his eye, and I wasn't sure whether to believe him. I shook my head.

"Look," he said, handing me the keys. "Take these. Sit in the back of the car. I promise we're going nowhere. You have to trust me."

Reassured, I slipped the keys into my pocket and climbed into the back seat. But the moment the doors were closed, the engine roared into life, and he shot off down the road.

"How did that happen?" I asked helplessly.

Everyone else was laughing, as if it was one big joke.

"I'm a mechanic, remember?" Pretos shouted, above the music. "I can start a car without the keys, no problem."

I laughed along although really I had no idea what he was talking about, or if he was telling the truth. And though I was secretly impressed at his skills, I dreaded being spotted by someone I knew. Worse, by my mother herself.

"Please, let me out," I pleaded. "If I'm late home I'll get grounded again. Please!"

Pretos swung the car around and back towards the park. I was home well before my curfew, but, as Mum smiled her approval, I felt a crackle of resentment and annoyance towards her. In my eyes, she had ruined my evening. In frustration, I stamped up to my bedroom and slammed the door closed. I wanted so much to go back out, to be with Glen and the others, instead of being stuck at home for another endless and boring night with my parents.

"What's wrong, love?" Mum asked, tapping lightly on the door.

"Leave me alone," I sulked.

I felt as though nobody understood me. Nobody except Pretos, Manny and Glen.

* * * *

For the next few days, Mum kept me busy with family visits and errands after school. When I was finally allowed out, I ran to the park and was red-faced and breathless by the time I arrived.

"Look who's here!" Glen grinned, slipping a proprietorial arm around me.

Pretos raised an eyebrow.

"You look stressed," he said. "You need to chill. Here…"

He passed me a joint and I took it and inhaled far deeper than I'd intended. After the initial coughing fit, I felt a pleasant fuzziness settling on me, like a warm blanket. I could no longer remember why I'd been so frustrated or resentful towards Mum. I could no longer remember a single problem I had.

"This stuff is lovely," I said.

We walked out of the park and down the road, and by the time we reached the turning at the bottom, I was stoned. I stopped, unsteady on my feet, and staggered back to sit on a bench. All of a sudden, I felt nauseous and dizzy. I closed my eyes and lowered my head carefully into my hands.

"I'm going to be sick," I mumbled.

"Just take a minute," Macie said, patting my back. "You'll be okay."

But then, I heard her shriek in alarm.

"That's your car!" she yelled. "Oh my God! Your mum and dad, Tina! They're coming down the road!"

I sat up, as though I'd had an electric shock. Sure enough, driving towards us was our family car, a distinctive burgundy Mondeo.

"Quick, lie down," Glen said to me. "We'll line up in front of you."

I slumped prone on the bench with my heart thumping. In front of me, forming a human shield, were Pretos, Manny, Glen, Macie and Caroline. I heard the car approaching and then, to my horror, it braked and slowed to a stop. There was the unmistakable sound of an electric window whirring down, before Mum's voice rang out in the evening air:

"Hi girls, have you seen Christina at all?"

Macie stifled a giggle.

"No, sorry," she replied primly. "I do believe she headed home earlier."

I held my breath, panicking that my feet were poking out at the end of the bench, or that the tell-tale green of Kerry football shirt was showing through the gaps in my make-shift fence. I heard Mum tutting and mumbling something to my Dad and then there was silence, hanging like a dead weight in the evening air. I felt as though time was slowing down, each second dragging by. Any minute now, I expected to see Mum's face, hands on hips, her red face glowering down at me. But breaking the silence, the window whirred again as it was closed, and the car slowly moved away. There was a collective breath out, a muted sigh of relief. But the moment they were safely out of sight, it was like deflating a balloon. We all burst out laughing, reliving the scene over and over, including Macie's over-formal reply.

"I do believe she headed home!" I scoffed. "That was hilarious!"

I still felt sick and light-headed, but I was high on more than cannabis. There was a camaraderie, like glue, binding me and my new friends together. It felt like harmless, innocent, fun. It felt like real friendship. It was, of course, nothing of the sort.

4

Innocence Lost

For two months, we continued to meet Pretos and the others in the park most afternoons after school. Sometimes, if we were playing truant, we'd meet them during the day, and Pretos might drive us up to the reservoir, or the canal, or to the snooker hall. There was a taxi rank near the snooker hall, and we were introduced to more men and more bottles of vodka and Jack Daniels. We were offered as much alcohol as we could drink and as much cannabis as we could smoke. And the best of it was, it was all free.

"You know I'm only a kid, right?" I'd told Pretos. "I can't pay for any of this stuff. I only get pocket money."

He had rolled his eyes and replied:

"Stop stressin'! You owe me nothing. Just enjoy!"

I couldn't believe how lucky I was. At school, the bullies were as relentless as ever, but these days I hardly noticed them. I wasn't in lessons much, and when I was, my mind was elsewhere. I had my own friends now, I had a boyfriend, I was drunk and stoned every afternoon. I knew how envious they'd be, if they knew the truth, and that gave me a new confidence and a secret smugness. On the outside, I was quiet and sullen at school. But inside, I was smiling. And smiling broadly.

Two months after I'd fallen in with the gang, Pretos met me after school and announced that we were going to a party.

"Wow," I beamed. "Sounds good."

In my mind, I was imagining buffet food and disco music and party clothes.

"What time does it start?" I asked.

Pretos sniggered a little and replied: "Anytime. You're the star guest."

He drove me to the bottom of my street so that I could nip in and get changed. Mum was working more late shifts, and Dad worked late every day, so I had my own door key now. With the party in mind, I got dressed into my Kerry shirt and my jeans and brushed my hair.

"Nice," Pretos said approvingly.

I was a little surprised when we arrived at the party house; just a run-of-the-mill council house on a nearby estate. There was no music blaring, no cars blocking the path, no balloons on the gate. We walked in, through a side door, straight into the kitchen. Immediately, the smell of cannabis was like an assault on my senses and the air was grainy with smoke. In the living room, some on sofas and some standing, there were around a dozen men, all of Asian heritage. All much older than me. I recognised Manny and Glen, and then a couple of girls around my age came in from another room. Gratefully, I made my way over to Glen and slipped my hand into his.

"Whose is this place?" I asked him.

"Belongs to Shaq," he said, pointing out an Asian man who was easily old enough to be my Dad. I felt a shiver of apprehension, but I swiftly bundled it aside. The house itself, apart from all the party guests, looked pretty normal. There were laminate floors and basic furniture and an ashtray spilling out onto a coffee table. My first thought was that Mum wouldn't have approved of that at all. I allowed myself a little giggle at the thought of Mum showing up here. She'd have more to complain about than the overflowing ashtray.

"Here," Pretos said.

He handed me a cracked mug with a drink that smelled like petrol, and I held my nose and downed the lot. It felt to me like the party was some kind of test and I didn't want to seem as though I couldn't hack it at this level. I wanted a passport into the gang; I wanted to be one of them.

Before long, there was a cannabis joint going round the room too. Then, someone popped a pill into the palm of my hand. Without question, I swallowed it down with a gulp of cheap vodka. As the music blared, I felt my heart beating, louder and stronger, in time with the bassline. Soon it was hammering, bursting right out of my chest and everything around me seemed suddenly, brutally, sharper. The colours shimmered and shone. A euphoric wave washed over me. But as soon as it came, it went. Now, everything was too sharp. The colours glared and dazzled and hurt my eyes. And my heart was banging so hard, I thought I'd collapse. All at once, I was shivering and shaking, with a line of cold sweat running down in between my shoulder blades. My shirt was sticking to me, and yet my hands were ice-cold.

The room started to spin and, as I clung onto the sofa, I realised I was going to be violently sick. Somehow, I managed to stagger out of the living room and up the stairs, in search of a bathroom. I hung over the toilet for what seemed like an hour, but it could just have been a few minutes. Then, on my hands and knees, I crawled through an open bedroom door and collapsed on top of the duvet of a single bed. Even with my eyes closed, I had to grip onto the sides of the bed, for fear of falling off. I drifted in and out of consciousness, hardly aware of where I was and wishing, fervently, that I was back home in my own Groovy Chick bed.

"Dad," I mumbled. "Feel sick."

Whenever I was ill, I wanted my Dad. But of course he had no idea where I was.

Time seemed to distort as I lay on the duvet; I'd no idea whether I'd been there for minutes or hours or even overnight. I felt so ill. One time I opened my eyes and Pretos was lying next to me. I could see his mouth moving but I couldn't work out the actual words. The blackness descended again, and the next time I woke up, Pretos was tugging at my jeans, pulling them down over my hips. I was conscious enough to realise that my underwear was being yanked off too, and I flinched and tried to struggle and yell out in protest. But I might as well have been tied up in knots; I felt paralysed. He said something but again, I couldn't make it out. And then, I slipped into numbness once more. Waking up, I saw Pretos, this time standing over me, at the edge of the bed.

"That was your first time, wasn't it?" he smirked.

Even through the fog, I knew exactly what he was talking

about. My jeans and underwear lay in a heap at the bottom of the duvet, and I felt horribly vulnerable and exposed. There was a stinging pain between my legs and spots of fresh blood. Worse still, deep inside in my soul, I felt gouged out, empty and alone. As though he had taken so much more than my virginity.

"Hey, Tina just raped me," I heard Pretos shout, as he walked back downstairs to join the others.

Somehow, I managed to scramble back into my jeans and after splashing my face with cold water, I stumbled downstairs, straight to the front door. When I found it was locked, I ran to the back door. Then, I tried the kitchen window. But everything was shut and locked. With panic rising like a tide in my chest, I rattled and pulled at the windows, but it was no use.

"Please, let me out," I pleaded. "I need to get home."

I was so disorientated that I wasn't even sure I was speaking out loud, or if anyone was listening. But then I heard the chink of keys behind me and the older man, Shaq, opened the door for me.

"Thank you," I gasped as I ran outside, inwardly cursing myself for thanking someone for the worst time of my life. Sobbing, tears blinding my eyes, I ran all the way home. I had vomit splattered down my shirt and my hair was soaked with sweat and tears.

"What's happened?" Mum asked, her face white with shock as she opened the door. "Look at the state of you, love. Where on earth have you been?"

"Leave me alone," I yelled, running straight up the stairs to the bathroom. "Just leave me alone!"

Later, still trembling and sobbing, I cuddled Vicky, my cat, as I lay on my bed and ignored Mum's pleas at the other side of my door.

"Let me in, Christina. I just want to talk to you."

Now, more than ever, I needed my family. Yet now, more than ever, I was pushing them away.

* * * *

The next morning, I still felt nauseous, there was a sharp stinging down below and I had double vision. Like a robot, I got dressed into my school uniform, straightened my tie, packed my pens and ruler, and went off to catch my bus. My heart plunged as I spotted Pretos' black Micra speeding down the street towards me.

"Get in," he demanded, through the open window.

I shook my head.

"I'm going to school," I replied.

"Get in," he insisted. I could hear the hiss in his voice.

I turned away, losing myself in the crowd of school kids at the bus stop. I didn't dare play truant that day. All of a sudden, in a bitter irony, school seemed like the safest place to be. All day, I felt sick with anxiety, knowing that however ghastly the party had been, my nightmare was not yet over. There was more to come. Pretos was waiting at the school gates at home time. This time, he jumped out of the car and grabbed my arm, pinching it hard.

"Get in the fucking car now," he snarled.

Shocked, I did as he said. There was another man in the

passenger seat, and I was bundled into the back like an awkward package or an unruly dog. My blood was pounding in my ears as Pretos screeched off down the road, leaving the other kids staring after us open-mouthed on the pavement.

"You know how much trouble you've caused?" he screamed. "Do you? You little slag?"

I sat, rigid with fear, whilst he yelled that he had wanted to take me for emergency contraception that morning. Because I wouldn't get in the car, at the bus stop, he'd sent another girl into the Family Planning Clinic to get the morning-after pill on my behalf. But his plan had backfired, when the nurse had made her swallow the contraceptive in front of her inside the clinic.

"So now, you're going to do as you're told. You're going to go into the fucking clinic and take the fucking pill. And Shaq is going to watch you do it."

My head was swimming. Nobody had ever spoken to me like this before. I had trusted Pretos. I had thought these men were my friends, that they were my way out of the bullying and the misery at school. How wrong, how misguided, how naïve, I had been. And I had never even heard of the morning-after pill, though I realised it was connected with the attack on me the day before.

As we drove, I tapped my left hand with my right, a nervous habit I'd always had. We arrived at the clinic, Shaq got out, and I followed. I didn't see that I had a choice. Inside, there was a receptionist, and also a nurse who was busy working in the background. As we waited to give our details, I felt a rush of relief, mixed with trepidation. Surely these professionals would realise that there was something wrong here. I was clearly not old enough to have sex, I was with a man old enough to be my father, who was obviously not my father, and I was here for emergency contraception. I was desperate for the nurse to ask me more questions, desperate to be found out. And yet, equally, I was desperate to get away with it and go home. I wanted both outcomes, and yet I wanted neither. The nurse handed me a plastic cup of water so that I could take the pill as she watched.

"All done," I said, handing the cup back.

Under Shaq's watchful eye, I listened to her instructions on what to do if I felt unwell.

"Do a pregnancy test in a week," she said.

And that was it. She turned her back and we went outside to where Pretos was waiting in the car. Thankfully, now, he seemed calmer.

"Get in and I'll drop you off at home," he offered.

I didn't dare refuse. Besides, I was more than an hour late home from school, and yet again I'd have some explaining to do to my parents. The sooner I got home, the better. I got into the back seat but he began driving in completely the wrong direction. I made a small sound of protest and Pretos whipped his head around from the driver's seat.

"Shut the fuck up!" he snarled.

I shrank back in alarm. How could I have thought that this man was my friend? He was completely different to the person he had been for those first two months. We arrived at the house where the party had taken place. Where the unthinkable had happened. Pretos took hold of my shoulder and marched me up the path, again through the side door. I couldn't believe that cars were driving past as normal and there was even a man walking his dog on the other side of the pavement. But nobody stopped. Nobody even seemed to notice me. And walking into the house, I had a merciless, paralysing flashback. The memories surged back; the music, the pills, the room spinning as I clung on.

'That was your first time, wasn't it...'

'Hey! Tina just raped me!'

I pulled myself back to reality. There was still a strong smell of cannabis, and there were empty vodka bottles on the floor, beside the back door. Reminders. A man I didn't recognise came in and smiled at Pretos.

"Is this her? The one you shagged?" he asked, nodding towards me.

"Yeah," Pretos replied. "And she loved it! She raped me!"

They both laughed and my cheeks burned with humiliation. They spoke about me as though I was an object, no feelings, no senses, something they'd found perhaps in a junk shop which turned out to be quite a bargain.

"You struck lucky there," the man grinned. "My turn next, eh?"

Then Glen poked his head into the kitchen and, though I moved towards him, he barely acknowledged me. As I stared, bewildered, he laughed along with Pretos and the other man.

'You are supposed to be my boyfriend!' I wanted to scream. 'Why are you not standing up for me? Why are you not angry with Pretos?'

But of course, I said nothing. I waited uneasily in the kitchen, aware of a growing tension, an expectation of sorts. It was as if they all knew something that I didn't. Then, three girls, a little older than me, burst in through the back door.

"Here she is!" laughed one. "Pretos' little slag. This is her."

I was just able to spot a quick nod from Pretos before I felt a punch right between my eyes, followed by another girl yanking my hair back, and a third kicking my shins. I fell to the floor, screaming, and curled into a ball, instinctively protecting my head. I had no chance against all three. My mobile phone fell from my pocket, and I saw it deliberately crunched underneath a black Nike trainer.

"Please!" I yelled. "Please stop!"

But the blows continued; punches, kicks, stamps. The pain was agonising. And I knew that Pretos, Glen and a couple of other men were standing by and watching it all happen. Nobody stepped in to stop the girls. Worse, they were offering words of encouragement and approval.

"Oh, see that kick, right in her stomach!"

My head was throbbing, and slowly, I felt myself losing consciousness. In terror, I wondered whether they might carry on kicking me until I was dead. I wondered if this was it for me. Mum and Dad might never find my body. Silent, hopeless tears leaked down the sides of my face. Then, the back door opened, and a voice bawled:

"What is going on? Look at all this blood in my fucking kitchen! Get her out!"

The attack stopped as quickly as it had started and I took my chance, staggering to my feet and out through the open door and into the street. My nose was pouring with blood and my eyes were already so swollen that I could barely see. Checking over my shoulder, I ran to the nearest house with a light on. I was terrified of them following me and giving me another beating. With my legs buckling, I hammered on the door.

"Help! Help!" I sobbed. "Please!"

An elderly gentleman answered, and the shock registered across his aged face. For a moment, I thought I had frightened him so much that he might shut the door on me. But then he offered me his arm and said kindly:

"Let's get you inside. What's happened to you, lass?"

Through my tears, I managed to give him my parents' phone number. They arrived within a few minutes and on our way to hospital, I whispered a cobbled together story about being mugged in the park.

"They took my phone," I stammered. "I'm sorry. I'm really sorry."

Mum put her hand over mine.

"You have nothing to be sorry for," she said firmly. "This is not your fault. We can get you a new phone, don't worry."

Her kindness just made me feel even more wretched. I wanted so much to tell her the truth, but how could I spill the whole story; the weeks and weeks I'd missed off school, the alcohol, the drugs, the party, the attack, the emergency contraception? It was all too much. I would be in so much trouble, and the shock would destroy my parents, I was sure of that. It was easier for me, and for them, if I lied about a mugging. And from now on, I would have nothing ever to

do with Pretos and his horrible mates again. My mind was
made up about that at least.

"I'm sorry," I muttered again.

At the hospital, I was treated for cuts and bruises, black
eyes and a broken nose. I had stamp marks on my back and
stomach, and I had a banging headache. Whilst Mum sat in
with me as I was being assessed, Dad called the police.

"What is the world coming to?" he said, shaking his head
as we were discharged. "What kind of monster would attack
a child in school uniform in broad daylight?"

They made such a fuss of me at home, bringing me hot
chocolate and a blanket so I could lie down on the sofa. Dad
dug out his *Only Fools and Horses* DVD and he and Mum
snuggled up either side of me. I felt like such a fraud. In my
mind, I felt it was all my fault. This had all started with me
playing truant and telling lies to my parents. I thought Mum
and Dad would be furious with me if they knew the truth. I
had no idea that I was the victim in all of this.

"You alright, pet?" Dad asked anxiously, tucking my
blanket around my feet. "Don't dwell on it. You're home
now and you're safe."

I nodded and stared, eyes glazed, at the television.

"I can't laugh, it hurts too much," I mumbled. "I'm fine,
though, really."

I didn't know how to tell him that I thought I'd never laugh
again.

****

A police officer came, the next day, to take a statement about the mugging. The details were sketchy for obvious reasons, but I blamed my poor recollections on my concussion.

"I think I may have blacked out at one point," I said. "I still have such a bad headache today. All I know is that a man in dark clothing stole my phone. I think he had a couple of others with him as well.

"I was on the floor with my eyes closed when they were attacking me, so I didn't really get a good look."

The policeman nodded and took brief notes. Part of me, again, wanted to scream out:

'Can't you see I'm lying? Why don't you challenge me?'

But the word just wouldn't come. The officer said he had very little to go off but promised to keep me in mind in case the mugger struck again.

"These people usually trip themselves up eventually," he said. "We'll get him in the end, I hope."

I doubted that very much, but again, I said nothing. For two days after the attack, with my face still swollen, I stayed off school. I spent the days in my bedroom, under my Groovy Chick duvet, with Vicky the cat curled up on the end of the bed, and with my childhood doll, Rosie, tucked in the crook of my elbow. As a little girl, I'd carried Rosie everywhere with me. Once, she'd even been posted off to the dolly hospital with a broken arm and I had cried theatrical tears every night until she was home again with her arm fixed. Now, aged 14, I felt I needed her more than ever. Propped up against my pillows, I examined my face in the mirror, and it seemed to me that my appearance had markedly changed beyond the bruises and the scratches; that the events of the party had been so damaging, so drastic, that I had changed outwardly too. I had gone into the party as one person and emerged as another. And though I looked like a child, as I huddled under my duvet with my faithful dolly, deep inside I felt a hundred years old. Internally, in my soul, I felt broken. Trapped between two worlds, I belonged in neither. I felt like I was treading water, just waiting, helplessly, for my head to go under. The uncertainty was terrifying.

And though I tried hard not to focus on the attack by Pretos, the memories bulldozed their way through the barriers of my consciousness. Slowly, inevitably, an acknowledgement of what had happened crystallised inside my mind. The word was tattooed onto the lining of my brain, as though I had been branded with a hot iron.

Rape.

I couldn't even say the word out loud. Couldn't admit it, even to myself. Was it rape? I had been unconscious, so did that count? I was a child. I had no idea. But the word squatted inside my head, refusing to budge, as cold and hard and uncompromising as a stone.

That evening, Dad came home from work, bringing a new mobile phone for me.

"Thanks Dad," I said guiltily, pushing away an image of my old one, smashed up on the laminate floor at the party house.

"Well, it wasn't cheap, but we need to know where you are," he said. "More important than ever now to keep you safe."

I nodded. I quickly messaged Macie and the rest of my pals, with my new phone number.

'Pretos has been looking for you,' she replied. 'You best get in touch. He even came to school at dinner break. You're in for it.'

My blood ran cold. What did he want with me? He had raped me, he had me beaten up, he'd drained me of every last shred of self-confidence and self-respect. Surely, he would leave me alone now? I reassured myself that he didn't have my new mobile phone number. But that evening, as we were eating, the house phone rang.

"Nobody there," Dad said, as he hung up. "Must be a wrong number."

A few moments later, it rang again.

"Same thing," he said. "Odd. Might be kids, messing about."

After the fifth silent call, he took the phone off the hook. Deep down, I was quaking. I knew exactly who was behind this. Sure enough, as I was watching the soaps with Mum, the doorbell rang.

"It's for you, pet," Dad called.

I went to the front door to find Macie and a couple of other girls.

"Are you coming out?" she asked.

"No way," I muttered. "Too late for me anyway. It's nearly dark."

"Look," she said in a hushed but urgent voice. "Pretos sent me. You had better come out. You don't want any trouble here."

I looked back, apprehensively, into the hallway. I could hear the *EastEnders* music floating through from the living room.

"Just be 10 minutes, Mum," I called. "Nipping the shop with Macie."

I walked out in the street, still in my red Minnie Mouse slippers. Pretos was parked at the end of the road. The little black Micra now seemed so malevolent; like a black cockroach scuttling down the street, pestering and scaring me. Filled with dread, I walked slowly towards the car.

"Get in," he said cheerfully, tilting his head at me. "Not you others, just Tina."

Wordlessly, I got into the passenger seat. My skin prickled with alarm. He drove off abruptly, onto the main road and past the park. A minute or so later, he turned into a quiet side street.

"Come on," he said, unbuckling his belt and unzipping his trousers.

I stared at him in confusion. I felt a mounting terror inside me.

"Blow job!" he snapped impatiently. "Come on!"

When I still didn't budge, he grabbed my head and forced it down in between his legs. I struggled not to gag and retch. It went on for what felt like hours. Strangely, all I could think was that I'd missed the soaps. Mum would be wondering where I was. I could feel my toes damp, through the end of my slippers, and cursed myself for not changing into my trainers. I focused on all these things. These safe, everyday, familiar things. Because my reality, my here and now, was too monstrous, too grotesque, for me to cope with.

Pretos groaned and abruptly shoved my head out of the way. It was over.

"Swallow it," he said. "Good girl."

I wiped my mouth and bit back on the tears as he drove me back home. At the end of the road, my mates were still milling about.

"Oh, Tina gave me a blow job," he announced, as I got out of the car. "Loved it, didn't you?"

Slowly, I walked back to my house, and it seemed to me my heart and soul were weighted down so much they were scraping on the pavement underneath me. I felt as though I had been scooped out and left hollow.

"Oh, you missed a cracking *EastEnders*," Mum beamed, when I walked back into the hallway. "What did you get from the shop?"

I mumbled something and ran upstairs, back to my Groovy Chick bedroom, back to my Rosie doll, back to my cat, back to my TV on the wall. Back to the girl I once was, but never would be again.

5

No Way Back

The morning after the sex act in Pretos' car, I went back to school, and on the bus my phone bleeped with a text:

'I will b outside school 4 u.'

I slammed my phone back in my pocket in frustration.

"How has he got my phone number? I've only had this phone for a couple of days."

Macie examined her hands before eyeing me shiftily.

"Sorry Tina," she said. "You know what he's like. I daren't say no to him. I had no choice."

Liquid terror slid through my veins as I imagined what Pretos might want with me. Would he force me to perform another sex act on him – or worse? I couldn't bear it. I slipped out of school at lunchtime to avoid him and went home, knowing Mum and Dad would both be at work. I felt pretty sure I could get away with it. I waited in my bedroom, with the lights off and curtains closed. I spoke to the cat in whispers, and didn't risk having the telly on, in case anyone heard it. I hardly dared to breathe.

"Quiet Vicky," I told her softly, stroking her fur. "We're hiding out, me and you."

For the first hour or so, everything was fine. But mid-afternoon, there was a rap on the door. I knew immediately who it was. I ignored it until the banging became so loud that I thought the neighbours might get annoyed and maybe even call my parents. There were two girls outside who I didn't recognise at all.

"Pretos sent me," said one, flicking her cigarette ash onto the doorstep. "You better get yourself out. Or else."

Unexpectedly, I felt a surge of defiance.

"Else what?" I snapped. "I'm not coming. Leave me alone."

I slammed the door in her face. I heard the girls walk away, giggling to each other. Minutes later, there was another knock. Then the doorbell chimed. Then the house phone started to ring. I put my hands over my ears.

"Leave me alone!" I yelled angrily.

I didn't know what to do. I felt persecuted. I went back upstairs and put my head under the duvet, trying to block it out. Eventually, the knocking and the ringing trailed off, and Mum and Dad arrived home from work. I made up more convincing lies about my day at school.

"Did a Maths test, went okay I think," I said.

"I'm glad you're working hard," Mum smiled.

As I was helping her chop vegetables ready for our evening meal, the house phone began ringing at the same time as the doorbell. I stood there quivering, momentarily frozen, whilst Mum marched towards the front door.

"No," I heard her say. "She's just busy at the minute. You can call back after tea if you like. Give us an hour."

She came back into the kitchen and wiped her hands on a tea-towel.

"I didn't like the look of those girls," she frowned. "Are they your new mates? They seemed a bit older than you. Too old, I think. No manners either."

I shook my head. I didn't really know where to start. The phone continued, shrill and insistent, and Mum sighed in exasperation before she went to answer it. There was a short pause before she said:

"Who on earth do you think you're talking to?"

She slammed the phone down furiously, but it rang again.

"Look, I've told you," she said firmly. "Don't call here again. Your language is filthy."

She came back into the kitchen and said to me:

"Do you know anything about these dirty phone calls?"

Lost for words, I flapped my hands, like a gasping fish. I was trying to look puzzled and confused, but it was so hard to hide the terror that seemed to be squeezing at my heart.

"Only, they were telling me they were going to do really disgusting things to my daughter," Mum continued. "They called me a racist word too. Is this anything to do with those girls from earlier? Or those men who gave you a lift the other week?"

"Oh no," I replied quickly. "Honestly, it's just a coincidence. And I told you, it wasn't me in that car. It was all a mistake."

"But how do they know I have a daughter?" Mum pressed. "And how do they know I'm white?"

"I don't know," I snarled. "Stop giving me the third degree. Okay?"

I went back to chopping carrots, as if the subject was closed. But my stomach roiled, and my hands shook. A few minutes later, the phone rang again, and though I tried to get there first, Mum snatched up the receiver just before me.

"Disgusting!" she yelled. "You filthy man! Don't ever call here again."

She turned to me and said: "They were threatening to do awful things to my daughter again. How do they know I have a daughter?

"I'm really spooked by this, Christina. I'm going to call the police if they ring again."

"Oh Mum, don't over-react," I said hurriedly. "It will just be idiots, messing about. They'll get fed up."

As soon as we had finished eating, I texted Pretos to let him know I was on my way. I didn't see that I had any other choice. I couldn't risk any more phone calls.

I met up with the usual crowd at the park and we crammed into the Micra. There was a second car too, with two strange men sitting in the front. We pulled up outside a house I didn't recognise and in the living room were three or four men lying back lazily on the sofas, smoking dope and drinking spirits.

"Sit next to me," said one, patting the space beside him.

It was an order, not an invitation, and I was fast learning how this worked. My whole body was stiff with protest and repulsion, but I did as I was told. The music was turned up and someone handed me a bottle of vodka. I took a gulp, grateful for anything to numb the foreboding that swirled inside me. Before long, I was drunk and stoned and thoughts of home seemed fuzzy and far away. I felt myself fading in and out of the room, but, as I came to, I was aware of one of the girls, on her knees, performing a sex act on one of the men. Everyone was watching, and there was a cheer all around the room when it was over. Even through the mist of drink and drugs, even though I'd had a brief insight into what Pretos was capable of, I was stunned and repulsed.

"Your turn next," Pretos said.

I shrank back as though I'd been stung.

"No," I slurred. "No, please."

My head was yanked back sharply by my ponytail.

"Yes," he seethed, so close to my face that a light spray of spittle settled on my cheeks. "Fucking do it."

A man I had never seen before unzipped his flies and pushed my head down onto him. Around me, everyone was clapping in a rhythm, as though it was the start of a race. I thought back, with a pang of longing, to my primary school races, to Mum and Dad clapping and cheering on the side-lines for the egg and spoon or the sack race. Now, I was being cheered to perform sex acts on men who were twice my age and more.

"Go Tina!" jeered one of the men. "All the way in!"

When it was over, I wanted to curl up and cry. But it was already someone else's turn, and so I just swilled the taste away with more vodka and took my place in the baying crowd. I went from punished, to punisher. I stepped so easily back over the line. I hadn't the courage or the conviction to stand up for this girl, just as she hadn't for me. We were all in this rotten mess together, yet we were very much on our own.

"Wahey!" yelled the men. "She's doing a good job. Not as good as Tina. Tina's the star, aren't you babe?"

I gave him a tight, uneasy smile. I was frightened of doing anything to make them angry and make me have to do it again. It was past 10pm when I got home and Mum was waiting up, in her nightie and dressing gown.

"Where the hell have you been?" she demanded. "We've been worried sick. Your phone is dead. I've been calling you. Your dad went out looking for you for over an hour. He searched everywhere."

I stumbled a little, as I stood in the doorway, my mind racing to grab at an explanation, a convenient lie.

"You're drunk!" she exclaimed. "I don't believe it! How can you be drunk? And on a school night!"

She marched to the bottom of the stairs and shouted:

"She's come home drunk!"

Dad came downstairs in his pyjamas, and I felt a pang of shame at keeping them both up when they worked so hard.

"You're in with a bad crowd," Mum remonstrated. "I don't like all these girls who keep coming to the door. They're too old for you. And they've such bad manners. I knew they were trouble the minute I saw them.

"It won't end well, Christina. Mark my words. What's happened to your old friends? Where are your friends from school? Why are you suddenly behaving like this?"

I hung my head. If only she knew.

"Well, you're grounded," she continued. "I'm taking your mobile phone. And I'm stopping your pocket money. You need to buck your ideas up."

I barely slept that night. The irony was, I wouldn't have minded being grounded one bit. But I knew I couldn't risk that. I was too scared of the gang now to try to defy them again. They owned me, to a certain extent. They certainly owned my time. I might as well have been a weary little stray, dragged around on a lead. I knew I'd have to find a way around the punishment.

And after the brutality of the rape and the oral rapes, I felt an unwanted but visceral connection with the men. I had shared something so violent and yet so intimate, so deeply personal. I didn't see any way back.

* * * *

The next few weeks passed in a string of so-called 'parties'; one blurring into the next through a haze of alcohol, cannabis, pills and trauma. I was regularly grounded and punished by my parents, but it made no difference. I was now answerable to people far more terrifying than they were. At the parties, I was usually made to have sex or to perform sex acts. Each time, I would gag and object or go stiff and still. Sometimes, involuntarily, I shouted out:

"No! Please stop!"

And I got a hard slap across the face for my impudence. Looking back, it was clear, it was painfully, blatantly, horribly, clear, that there was no consent. I was a child, more often than not wearing my school uniform, and the gang members were all aware of that too. Often removing my school tie was the first act before it all began.

Most days, I skipped school, or I met up with Pretos and his mates in the afternoons. I had quickly accepted that I had no choice; if I didn't do exactly as they said, I'd be battered and beaten. The memory of the attack after the rape was fresh in my mind and felt as though it always would be. I'd seen them kicking and punching girls who refused to perform sex acts. I'd had a few slaps across the face as payback for a moment's hesitation before an oral rape.

And there was always the explicit threat that they would tell my parents what I was up to, if I didn't do as they said. If I missed just one party, or ignored just one call from Pretos, he'd send someone to my home to look for me. He was always careful to send girls to the house; never one of the men, so that my parents never actually saw them in person. Or he'd call our landline, screaming vile racist abuse and sexual threats at my mother down the phone. I didn't want him to have any contact with her. Part of me was frightened he would tell her what he wanted with me but a bigger part worried that he might hurt her too. That foreboding was always there, lingering in my stomach like a sickness.

At 14, I didn't understand that I was doing nothing wrong. Looking back, of course, the best thing would have been to tell my parents. I was a victim. I was being groomed, exploited, brainwashed. I was being sexually assaulted, beaten up and raped. Yet the gang managed to make me feel that this was all my fault; whether this was well thought out manipulation on their part, or whether they had no definite framework, I would never know. But they were confident I'd never dare confide in my parents. I didn't even realise, at that point, that it *was* abuse and it *was* rape. I didn't want it to happen. But often I was too frightened to speak out. So perhaps I was culpable, maybe I had to bear some responsibility? As a child, spiralling into an alien world, I was all too quick to blame myself.

And despite the coercion, and the fear, there was a strange and ambiguous pleasure in being part of the gang. I have to be completely honest and say that there was an illicit thrill and an excitement attached to the membership. The sense of belonging and acceptance was everything to me. I had spent month after month cowering away from the school bullies, eating solitary lunches in the canteen, moping around the corridors on my own. At last, I was a part of something, and it mattered less what it actually was.

I had bragging rights now, in the schoolyard. I went from being a bullied kid without mates to showing off about my older friends and boyfriends. I had free access to ecstasy, alcohol and cigarettes. I rode around in cars with men five, 10, 20 years my senior. For a 14-year-old, struggling for a foothold in the school hierarchy, the situation brought with it an impressive level of notoriety. I gloried in that, naively and foolishly, without thinking of where it would lead. Like any teenager, I didn't think ahead. I saw only what was in front of me.

I didn't feel I could say no to Pretos, but then, I didn't always want to say no either. I wanted the vodka and the drugs and I wanted the excitement and the feeling of living on the edge. I didn't want the physical and sexual abuse, but I was beginning to accept that it was part of the package.

I hated what happened at the parties. I loathed the sexual assaults, though in my mind, back then, I didn't see them as such. I couldn't allow myself to think like that. And I was able to block them out, a lot of the time, with booze and pills. I was trapped in a vicious and suffocating circle and one which suited Pretos perfectly; I needed substances to help mask the effects of the abuse, and my abusers were ones who supplied the substances.

"Here," he'd say. "You look stressed. Have a joint."

I didn't see it then. But he was reeling me in, just like a tiny fish. And as I got used to ecstasy tablets, or 'Chickers' as we called them, I loved them. They were like sweets, all different colours with cute little girly emblems on the top, sometimes a cherry, a Shrek, or a Nike tick. Pretos always had a big bag of them, he called them 'Smarties' and he'd hand out up to five at a time.

"Have another one," he'd say, slipping the tablets from his sweaty hand into mine.

By the end of the night, I was so spaced out and often found myself dancing down the street, all on my own, humming the *Emmerdale* theme tune, in love with the entire world. I was too drugged up most of the time to think about the sickening reality of what was actually happening to me. Instead, I felt important and liberated and in-the-know. I felt like a girl who was making her own choices, doing her own thing. I definitely didn't feel like a victim.

Most nights, I stayed out later than I was allowed. I'd stagger in through the front door to be met by my mother in her dressing gown, hands on hips, her face red with fury.

"Why are you putting us through this?" she demanded. "What's happening to you?"

I was either too stoned or too high to even formulate a reply. She and Dad were no more gullible than other parents, but they had no experience of Class A drugs. They didn't know what to look out for, and didn't suspect for a moment that I was taking anything other than too much alcohol. We had neighbours who smoked cannabis and so I could simply shift the blame onto them if Mum questioned the smell. I managed to waft away their concerns as easily as if it was smoke from a joint.

"You two need to calm down," I told them. "I'm fine, everything's fine."

But the worry was a constant presence in our house. My parents worked long hours, Mum worked unsociable shifts, and they couldn't keep me under constant supervision. At 14, I was too old to be babied.

"Is it the mugging?" Mum asked me. "You haven't been yourself since you were attacked in the park that night. I don't want you to worry about that Christina, you're safe now."

"Right," I nodded, but inside, I was laughing bitterly. I had never felt less safe in my entire life.

At night, when I was late home, Mum and Dad would drive around searching for me, but by now I had left the park and the local streets behind, and I was hidden away in grotty houses, at dubious parties and with so-called friends, and they had no idea where to look for me.

"You're in with a bad crowd," Mum kept saying. "You need to buck your ideas up, young lady. You're going to fail all your GCSE exams at this rate!"

She tried taking my mobile phone away, as a punishment for my behaviour, but I just got another from one of the men. Pretos had an endless supply of mobile phones and I never thought to question where they came from.

"Thanks," I'd smile, as he handed me yet another handset.

I thought he was so generous. And it felt wonderful to stroll casually into school with the latest model of phone in my trouser pocket; it was something else to build up my reputation and it was more ammunition against the bullies. It never occurred to me, back then, that providing me with a phone was the gang's way of controlling me and tracking me.

Mum stopped my pocket money too, but I had access to unlimited amounts of junk food, cigarettes, booze and drugs – and it was all free. And so, I didn't much care whether I got pocket money or not; the phrase itself seemed outdated and somehow no longer applicable to me. I had left my childhood, and all that was in it, way behind.

I was often grounded also, but there were several evenings when my parents were working, and it was easy for me to slip out without permission. Other nights, I'd play my music so loudly, and scream back at Mum in arguments, until she flung her hands up in the air in helpless defeat and yelled:

"That's it! I can't take any more!"

I grabbed my chance to sneak out of the house whilst she was crying. Though my own eyes were dry, I felt her tears running through me too, soaking me with her sadness and her desperation.

"It's the wrong crowd," she kept repeating. "They're leading her astray."

My parents had no idea I was being groomed and neither did I. This was 2005, it was some years prior to the media storm surrounding child sexual exploitation and grooming. Besides, I was a nice kid, from a nice home, in a nice area. Nobody suspected anything sinister. Those things just didn't happen, and especially not to girls like me.

6

Downward Spiral

One Sunday afternoon, Pretos and the gang ordered me to meet them, and then announced we were off to a party. We arrived at a block of flats I didn't recognise, on the outskirts of Huddersfield. It was a dingy place, a real dump, with a horrible rotting smell coming up through the floorboards. Immediately, I covered my nose and started to complain.

"You do as you're told," Pretos said shortly. "Here, take this."

He handed me a pill and a bottle of vodka. There was another man there whose name and nickname I didn't know, who motioned with a meaty hand for me to sit next to him. I was slowly picking up that the gang all had bizarre and slightly malevolent nicknames. There was Beastie, a hairy man, with a beard and spots underneath the growth. There was one man who had bad, yellowing teeth and a square head whose name seemed to change each time I met him. He was a bit ghoulish in appearance and gave me the creeps. There was Manny, Little Manny, Glen, Dracula or Drac, Finny, Kammy, Big Riz, Raj, Boy, Nurse, Vic, Fish, Faj, Chiller, Mosabella, Shaq, Bully, Junior and Kid. Of course there was also Pretos. Some who shared similar names or derivatives were brothers or cousins. I thought it was comical and confusing at the time. It's only looking back that I realise it was all part of the plan and that they didn't want me and the other girls to know their real names. Their aim was to make it as baffling and incomprehensible as possible, so that if I ever tried to identify them formally, I'd struggle.

Today, with this man waving a fat finger at me, I had a sinking feeling that I was going to be forced to give him some kind of sexual favour.

"Look, I'm due at my gran's for tea later," I said, still gagging on the smell. "Mum will hit the roof if I'm late. I can't stay long."

Pretos and the man laughed, as if that only added to their enjoyment. The time ticked by quickly and, despite the floaty effects of the drugs, I began to feel edgy.

"I can't let my gran down," I pleaded. "Please let me go."

The man ran his eyes over me, and his tongue lolled out a little. His long, lank hair hung by his ears, like two greasy curtains. He had a huge belly, straining over the waist of his jogging pants and across his face, like a slug trail, was a glistening layer of saliva. I felt my insides flipping and recoiling.

"Come here," he coaxed; his voice barely more than a rasping whisper. "Come on."

It was more menacing and chilling than if he had shouted at the top of his voice. I was a lamb being tricked into the back of a slaughter lorry.

"I need to go," I protested weakly. "My gran is cooking for me."

But he was already unzipping his trousers. Pretos laughed mirthlessly and pressed 'record' on his phone. There was nothing I could do; I knew he was filming me but my head was firmly held in place by the man's sweaty hands. Afterwards, Pretos insisted that I watched the recording.

"Don't stress," he said, seeing me cringe as I followed the images. "You look good. You did a good thing. You can go home now. Good girl."

I wiped my mouth with my sleeve, and it left a stain on the cuff. Pretos dropped me on the street near my gran's and I ran in, ready with another well-polished lie about how Macie and I had lost track of the time.

"Sit down, love," Gran said kindly, putting the gravy boat down next to the roast potatoes.

It felt surreal, sitting around the table with her and my parents, eating roast chicken and Yorkshire puddings, with the foul taste and smell of the man still strong on my skin. It seemed to me as though my two worlds were so diametrically opposed that one surely must not be real. The world of sex acts and drugs and Asian gangs did not, could not, exist. But then, as Gran brought out apple pie and custard, I spotted the stain on my cuff. I remembered, with a shudder, how my head was forced down by the man, how Pretos had laughed, how he had saved the film into a file on his phone. And I knew it was horribly real.

"You alright my love?" Gran asked. "You look peaky."

I forced a roast potato down and smiled weakly.

"Just a bit tired," I said. "Sorry, I'm not that hungry."

The irony was, with the stress of this new secret life, and my drug-induced loss of appetite, I was starting to lose weight. Soon, the school bullies would have no reason to taunt me. I'd be the same size and weight as everyone else. But I was past caring.

As we were driving home, that evening, I got a text from Pretos telling me to meet him at the park.

'Can't,' I replied. '2 late 4 me.'

'B there,' he replied. 'Or else.'

My insides lurched horribly. I was becoming accustomed to feeling afraid, to dreading the next hour, the next day.

"I need to go out," I said to Mum. "Just getting the bus to Macie's. Homework trouble."

She rounded on me.

"Absolutely not," she replied, already fired up for battle. "You're going nowhere. You've been out once today and it's getting late. You have school in the morning."

I glared at her, more in despair than anger.

"Please," I pleaded. "Not for long. I need to go."

But Mum stood firm. And Dad, in the background, his voice typically soft, but weary, said:

"Just leave it for tonight, pet," he said. "Listen to your Mum. She knows best."

I threw my arms up. The unease rushed through me like a torrent of water. I was under so much pressure, and I didn't know how to cope with it. I had no outlet, no solutions. I waited until they were both watching TV and then, after another angry text from Pretos, I pulled on my trainers and disappeared out of the back door.

'On my way,' I texted.

I knew my parents would be furious. Worse still, they would be worried sick. But that was nothing compared to what I would face if I defied Pretos and the gang.

I was a slave – to them – and to myself.

* * * *

Late one morning in spring 2005, I was skipping school as usual, hanging around the bus station in my school uniform, waiting for one of the gang to turn up with the car. Macie and I had just found an empty bench to sit on when, to my dismay, I spotted my gran in the bus station café opposite. She was with another lady, and they were both sitting down to a coffee and a bun.

"Oh no," I groaned.

Before I could duck down, Gran looked up, straight at me. Her expression changed from one of surprise and pleasure to evident consternation, when she realised I was supposed to be at school. As she stalked out of the café towards me, leaving her coffee and bun behind, I took the easiest option, and I turned and ran.

"Come on!" I yelled to Macie. "We need to get out of here!"

We both legged it back towards the main entrance, through the doors, and into the sunshine.

"She won't catch us," I said breathlessly. "She has a bad hip."

But I knew that wasn't the end of it. And that afternoon, Mum was waiting for me when I got home, drumming her fingers on the kitchen work surface.

"Your gran saw you at the bus station," she said. "You've been playing truant. What have you got to say for yourself?"

I shrugged as innocently as I could.

"I don't know what you're on about," I replied. "I was in school. Gran must be getting mixed up."

Mum continued to tap her fingers and it felt ominous, a portent of trouble ahead.

"Gran needs new glasses," I added insolently.

Mum puffed out her cheeks with a long-suffering sigh.

"Well, we'll see who's telling the truth, because I have an appointment with your deputy head tomorrow."

My heart sank. So far, amazingly, I had got away with playing truant without so much as a reprimand at school. As long as I registered in form, so that I was officially present, nobody had noticed that I was leaving immediately afterwards. It had been going on for months, and I had become bolder and braver as the days went by. Pretos had even started waiting right outside school for me, in his black Micra. The teachers didn't once question who he was or why he was there. And neither did they question why I was missing from every single lesson every day. As long as I had a tick in the register, as long as I was virtually present, all was well.

Until now.

"You don't need to go into school," I babbled. "It's a waste of time. You'll miss work too. If I was absent, school would call you. You know that."

But Mum's mind was made up. I could tell she didn't believe me. And the next day, after her meeting with my teachers, she was standing at the school gates, with a face like thunder.

"Your teachers all said that you haven't been in lessons," she said. "You're marked in on the register but then nobody can remember seeing you after that. I looked at your exercise books and they're nearly empty! You haven't done any classwork for weeks. Where have you been? I want the truth!"

My mind was working fast. I mumbled a half-baked story about nipping off to go shopping or dilly-dallying around the bus station.

"I haven't been doing any harm," I said. "I promise. I was being bullied at school. I get teased for being overweight and I can't take it anymore. They just won't leave me alone. I hate school and I didn't know what to do.

"I've just been hanging around the shops or sitting in the bus station with a Lucozade. Honestly. It's been really hard, Mum, with the bullying. I'm sorry."

It had started with a half-truth, but then I was getting in deeper and deeper. I was building a rickety tower of lies, with such shaky foundations that it would inevitably come crashing down around me.

"You should have spoken to me," Mum said gently. "I could have helped with the bullying, love. We should have spoken to school. I'm your mum. You can tell me anything."

I nodded, uncertainly, knowing there was no way I could tell her what was really going on.

Mum was thankfully more annoyed with the school than with me, for not noticing that I had been absent for so long. She and Dad contacted the Diocese of Leeds, to make a complaint.

"It's just not good enough," she said. "They should have let me know that you were playing truant. Instead, the months have gone on, and now you're in with a bad crowd. And you're way behind with your schoolwork."

The summer holidays were approaching, and she and Dad decided I should move schools the following academic year.

"You need a new start," she said. "I've applied for a job in the office at your new school, so it means I can keep an eye on you whilst I'm at work.

"So you can forget any ideas about messing around on the bus station all day. You need to knuckle down now. No more truancy. No more lies. It's over.

"Back to normality."

Deep down, I wished so much that she was right. But I had a horrible feeling that it would take more than a new school to get my life back to how it once was.

* * * *

In the long summer holidays which followed the end of Year Nine, my behaviour plunged downwards. As surely as if I had picked at a thread and pulled, my life began to unravel at a dizzying pace.

Each day began with a text from one of the gang, telling me when and where we were meeting up. I was drinking, smoking weed and taking pills on a daily basis. We were driven to houses and flats all around Huddersfield and more often than not, I missed my curfew for being home.

"I'm not standing for this!" Mum said, as I stumbled in through the front door, glassy-eyed and over an hour late, yet

again. "You need to start coming home earlier, young lady."
I laughed mirthlessly. She spoke as though I had any choice
in this; as though it was my decision to go out each day with
a gang who plied me with drugs and sexually abused me.

But I couldn't admit or understand what was happening,
even to myself. So I couldn't begin to explain it to her. Instead
I rolled my eyes scornfully, and said:

"Yeah, yeah."

Mum grounded me and confiscated my mobile phone, as a
punishment, and was baffled when I simply shrugged indif-
ferently. I knew Pretos would have a new one waiting for
me the following day; maybe even an updated model in the
latest colour.

The next morning, I waited until she and Dad had gone to
work, and then I sneaked out of the house.

"I have no idea what to do with you," Mum sobbed, when
I rolled home again late the following day, again drunk out
of my mind.

That was the problem. I had no idea either.

One day, at the snooker hall, Pretos said to me:

"Nurse wants you to go for a walk with him along the
canal."

I shuddered. Nurse was in his late teens and I had no idea
how he'd come by his grim nickname. I didn't want to go.
But I also knew I had no choice. When I hesitated, Pretos
pushed his face into mine and whispered:

"I've been keeping you topped up with cigs and vodka for
months. Remember that. You owe me."

The canal ran along the back of the pool hall and was not

far from the taxi rank where some of the gang liked to hang out. There were a couple of 'party houses' in that area too.

"Come on," Nurse said, jerking his head towards the door.

We walked outside, onto the canal path, and the air was thick with the tension between us. I wanted to speak, to lessen my own anxiety, but my mouth was dry. I felt as though I was walking towards the electric chair.

Though my angst was horribly real, it made no sense to me. I felt trapped and yet we were in the fresh air, there were paths winding in all directions, and of course I could have run away at any point. I wasn't in chains or handcuffs. Nurse didn't even have a hand on my shoulder. Yet the hold he had over me was stronger than that. I was hostage to him and worse, to myself. I knew, from the other girls, that Pretos always asked for feedback from the men he set them up with, and then he would dole out either praise or punishment, depending on the report. I'd seen enough girls with black eyes and bust lips – not to mention the ones I'd received myself – to know that positive feedback was important. I tried to smile at Nurse but it came out as more of a grimace.

We soon reached the steps, and walked down to the canal side, mostly out of sight from the road. There was a bench there too. My heart was beating faster now. When we got to the bottom step, Nurse turned to face me. He said something but my heart was clattering so loudly against my ribs, pounding in my ears, that it blocked out his voice. As his mouth came towards me, I recoiled on instinct. His breath stank and his eyes, close up, were watery and fish-like. I let out a small, pleading squeal of protest, but if Nurse heard, he certainly didn't show me any mercy.

"Take this off," he muttered, tugging at the buttons on my top.

I was fearful in case anyone saw us. But equally I was desperate for someone to challenge us. Nurse forced me up against the stone wall and shoved his hands into my knickers. Squeezing my eyes tightly shut, I tried to project myself five, 10 minutes into the future. This would be over soon, I told myself. I would be walking home in a matter of minutes.

"Just hang on," I told my inner self. "Just hang on."

Nurse smirked when he was done with me and walked back up the stone steps, leaving me behind. I sank to my knees, at the side of the bench, gagging against the stench of the dirty canal water but more against the sheer white horror of the assault. I made my way back to the snooker hall, back to my abusers, back for more punishment and more trauma. It made no sense to me then and it makes no sense to me now. I was like a robot, completely dominated and under their control. I had lost all of my self-esteem and self-confidence, and with that all ability to make my own decisions had gone. I might as well have been operating on remote control.

"Here she is," Pretos smiled. "Well done."

And despite everything, I glowed under his praise. He offered me a swig of vodka and congratulated me on my performance with Nurse. His words meant so much to me. I was like a little flower, turning my face to his sun for warmth. I loathed him, I was terrified of him, yet I was desperate for his approval. I was desperate to be included in the gang.

It was another paradox, another contradiction which only added to my turmoil and anxiety.

"My favourite girl," Pretos said indulgently.

"Thanks," I said, and I drank in the affirmations, despite the fact that I was shaking violently. Hours later, I was still trembling when I got home, mid-evening, to find Mum packing the big family suitcase.

"Your dad's booked the ferry," she smiled. "We're off to Ireland next week."

It was as though she had thrown a warm and snuggly comfort blanket over me.

"Really!" I beamed. "Really?"

County Kerry was, to me, like a mythical land, a perfect utopian refuge, the only place where I would be truly safe from the evils in Huddersfield. It felt like the answer to all of my problems. I imagined myself running across the beach, collecting shells, watching films with my cousins. And already, my shivering was easing. Already, there was hope ahead.

As if she was reading my mind, Mum said:

"I think it's just what you need. You have to get away from this new crowd, Christina. They're a bad influence, those older girls. When you get home from Ireland, it's a new school and a new start for you. I don't want to hear anything more about this new crowd. You hear me?"

I nodded. I was so thrilled to be going on holiday, I was prepared to think anything was possible.

Out on deck on the ferry, the sea air was sharp and bracing, despite the summer weather, and I felt more alive than I had for months.

"This is perfect timing for you," Mum said, as the wind blew our hair into our faces. "You need a holiday. I know you like your freedom at home. But you'll love it, seeing your cousins, just wait and see."

And she was right, too. The fortnight we spent in Kerry was blissful. Mum and Dad had insisted that I left my mobile phone at home, so that I didn't spend the holiday texting my mates. It had been the same rules ever since I'd got a phone, aged 11, and so there was no room for argument or compromise.

"It's a different network over there," I'd told the gang. "Nothing I can do. My relatives live in the middle of nowhere and there's no signal either."

Pretos accepted that grudgingly.

"You make sure you call me, the minute that ferry gets back," he ordered.

"I will," I promised.

And it was such a release, during those two weeks, knowing that the gang was on the other side of the Irish Sea. Knowing that they couldn't order me about or track me down. Knowing I did not have to perform sex acts on strangers.

"I feel like I've got my daughter back this week," Mum laughed, ruffling my hair as we walked along the seafront with ice-creams. "You're a different girl when you're over here."

I smiled happily in agreement. I felt lighter and more upbeat in every way. And it was only whilst I was away from the gang that I began to realise just how much they had taken over my life, treating me, at times, worse than an animal. Worse than an object.

"What I don't understand is, how you went from good to bad, with nothing in between," Mum continued. "It seemed to happen overnight. What was it? What made you change like that?"

I didn't reply. I knew she was perplexed by the sudden downslide and then the equally sudden upturn, in my behaviour. But I didn't even want to think about going back home. I wanted to wish the whole thing away; my home, my school, my friends and most of all, Pretos and his gang. Yet I suspected, the moment I landed back in Huddersfield, the switch would happen again, just as quick, just as brutal. From good to bad, with nothing in between.

7

Trapped in Hell

For my 15th birthday, my parents bought me clothes and new trainers and took me out for a slap-up meal, both in the morning and the evening. Dad and I had a special fondness for a Wetherspoon breakfast and we enjoyed a full English on the morning of my birthday with extra buttery toast.

"Delicious," Dad smiled, as he mopped up his egg yolk with his crusts.

Later, at home, we celebrated with a birthday cake and more presents. I was still a child, still a little girl at heart. I still loved to blow out candles, to rip open wrapping paper, to feel the nurturing love and affection of my parents.

Yet, at 15, I had had sexual contact with hundreds of men, many of whom I had never met before or since. Mostly, I had no idea of their names, their ages, or their addresses. I estimated there were around 300 men in total so far, yet it was impossible to know for sure.

It was a big secret to carry around and I felt like I was sitting on a time-bomb. As I went through the motions; opening gifts, eating cake, hugging my parents, I felt like a fraud. What would they say if they knew? Would they disown me, throw me out? I didn't think so. But I did think they would be upset and furious and disappointed. And I did not want to be the cause of all of that.

"Sure you don't want a new duvet cover?" Mum asked, as she came in to kiss me goodnight after my birthday meal. "You've had that Groovy Chick set since you were small. It's looking washed out now and you've outgrown it."

I shook my head firmly.

"I want to keep it," I protested. "I love it. Please don't change it."

It was my way of hanging onto the little girl I used to be. But I was clinging on with my fingertips. I was so terrified of losing her completely.

With my birthday celebrations over, I began Year 10 at a new school, where Mum now worked also, as an office assistant. For me, as for any teenager, it was a double blow. Much as I hated the bullies at my own school, it was a big challenge to try to start again at a new place. And knowing that Mum was watching me like a hawk, making sure I was in class, making sure I didn't so much as look out of a window without permission, just added to the stress. I was under pressure too from the gang to skip school and go to parties, and the two opposing and antagonistic sides of my life weighed very heavily on me. Those first few weeks were so demanding and oppressive that I thought of little else.

"I want to see your school books at the end of each day," Mum told me. "I want to know that you're in class and you're working hard."

"Yeah," I mumbled. "No problem."

Her concern was well-meaning, but I felt crushed by it. And then Pretos chipped in with his demands:

'U betta be outside school at 2pm,' he wrote. 'I will b there. Takin u to a party!'

I was stuck in the middle. There was no compromise, no middle ground. These two paths were parallel and mutually exclusive, and I wrestled mentally with my dilemma, day after day.

'U best be there,' Pretos reminded me. 'Or else.'

And so, it was easier of course to let Mum down than it was to defy Pretos, and slowly, as she settled into trusting me again, I began finding devious ways around her plan.

Her shift in the office finished soon after lunch, and so I worked out that I could attend my morning lessons, hang around over the lunch break, making myself obvious and visible to the teachers, but then walk out before the afternoon session began. I was so devious and practised at truancy now, that I managed it without too many complications.

There was even a police officer on site at school, yet she could not keep track of my movements either. She had called me into her office for a chat more than once.

"If you have anything on your mind, you can tell me," she offered. "I know you had an issue with truancy at your old school, and we need to address that. It might seem harmless to you but skipping class can lead to more serious problems."

I widened my eyes innocently.

"Oh no, nothing like that," I convinced her. "I just hung out at the bus station when I wasn't in class. I don't skip school anymore; I'm working hard now."

I managed to con her, as I did my teachers, as I did my parents. As a child, I saw it as a real achievement, as something to brag about. Now, I look back and see that I was only really conning myself.

Coming out of school, I'd walk down an alley called 'Monkey's Neck', to meet the groomers who were parked up and waiting for me on the main road. Sometimes, I'd hear Dad's rumbling pickup truck on the road and would have to run and hide from him. I'd collapse into a heap of helpless giggles behind the nearest bus shelter or a road sign, as he trundled past, oblivious.

"Got away with that one," I'd tell Pretos as I jumped into his car, breathless.

And yet a part of me, a very small part, longed for Dad to spot me and find out what I was up to. I went to so much effort to keep my secrets. Yet I wanted them to be discovered too. I needed to be exposed. It was yet another confliction, another incongruity in the chaos of my day-to-day routine.

Other times, Pretos would wait for me right outside school, quite brazenly. He didn't seem to care that my teachers or my classmates, or even my mother, in the school office, might see him and confront him. And as it was, nobody ever seemed to challenge him. Ever.

"I'm untouchable," he'd tell me and he said it with such authority that I believed it.

And because I was at a new school, with a new set of kids, he began putting me under pressure not only to attend parties myself, but also to recruit new girls for him.

"Must be some pretty girls in your new class?" he coaxed.

"We've got plenty of vodka to go around. Why don't you hook us up? Get me some numbers babe, there's a good girl."

I wanted to please him. But it wasn't that simple. I had yet to make firm friendships myself, in my new school, before I could then introduce them to Pretos. And that lack of security, amongst my peers, served only to push me even further into the clutches of the gang. I had nobody else to turn to. I was reliant on the vodka, the cigarettes and the cannabis. But I was also reliant on Pretos and his gang. The lifestyle they offered, the demands they made, were as much of an addiction as the alcohol and the drugs. It was all bad for me. It would all kill me, if I didn't stop it. Yet I could not break free. And so when I spotted Pretos' Micra, outside school, my heart plummeted and soared all at once. I was muddled, emotionally and psychologically, to the point where I did not know what I wanted. I was too confused to think for myself.

"Come on," he'd say, his eyes glinting as he patted the passenger seat. "There's a party on!"

As I think back, I can now see that 'party' was an appallingly cruel euphemism for a living hell. Many of the party houses were only partially decorated and furnished. There was an obligatory leather sofa in most of the living rooms and grubby mattresses in the bedrooms. One house in particular had concrete stairs which led up to a dingy bathroom, and I was often dragged into there, by one or more of the gang, and made to perform whatever outrage they demanded of me.

There was no shortage of drugs and alcohol and cigarettes, and I was fast becoming dependent on all three. By now I had built up a better tolerance to cannabis and ecstasy and I accepted everything on offer, knowing it would give me a buzz, but more importantly understanding it would dull the pain and the horror of what was to come. Taking the pills was helping me to lose more weight, because they suppressed my appetite, and it was ironic that now, after moving schools, I had at last found a way to slim down and silence my bullies. But at what cost?

Sometimes, the men would slip pills into our drinks, slyly, so that we were out cold after a few sips. They saw that as just a bit of fun. I woke up on more than one occasion with the distinct sense that I had been sexually assaulted, but without knowing who was responsible and what exactly he, or they, had done to me.

At the first few parties, in those early months, the sex acts were confined mostly to the bathrooms, and mainly it was with one man at a time. That in itself seemed horrific, but I would later look back on those days and wish that we could rewind to such simplicity. In the twisted view of the gang, it was tame and almost reasonable for a girl to be forced to have sex in private with just one man. As the months passed, it became the norm for us to be ordered to perform sex acts in front of a crowd and on various different men in the room.

New girls would arrive, shy and awkward, standing in the doorway and no doubt wishing they could somehow melt into the walls. I recognised the apprehension in their eyes only too well. But after a handful of Chickers, they'd be dancing around the room, throwing off their clothes and squawking with laughter as they were dragged off to the bedrooms; little more than carcasses. Later still, there was a third transformation, most disturbing of all, as they emerged from the bedrooms, like frightened little animals, crawling out from under a rock, with black, haunted eyes, tramlines of smudged make-up and their faces etched indelibly with trauma and shock.

"Okay?" I asked. "Sure you're okay?"

They nodded, always. Because what was the point in complaining? There was no way around it, because if we refused to do exactly as we were told, we were threatened and beaten. And if we refused the drugs, we were simply force-fed. I'd had it done to me more than once. One man would hold open my jaw, the other would pour in the tablets. And that way, I had to take far more at once than I wanted and definitely far more than was safe. It was better just to do as I was ordered in the first place and swallow whatever drugs I was offered. Once, after forcing me into having sex, one of the gang bought me a pizza.

"Here," he smiled, handing me a box with a greasy meat feast pizza inside. He took a slice for himself and the melted cheese dribbled down his chin. Though I hadn't eaten for ages, and my stomach was empty, I had no appetite and I had to force the pizza down. It tasted oily and nasty, and it was almost cold; a depressing metaphor.

"Thanks, it was lovely," I said, wiping my mouth and wishing I could clean my teeth.

I felt coated, head to foot, with grease and slime, so dirty and grimy, as though a hundred showers and baths would not get me clean again. And for years afterwards, I couldn't help dwelling on the memory of that pizza. It felt like a low amongst lows, a symbolic nadir. I'd swapped my dignity, my self-respect, my innocence, for a greasy pizza which I didn't even enjoy.

* * * *

Pretos seemed to be in charge, certainly of our little group, and he gave out all the orders. He set up girls with other men and he also arranged many of the parties. Though he was not the oldest gang member, he had an incomprehensible yet iron-like hold over everyone. I had no idea what made him the boss, and I appreciated it was not my place to question it.

At one party, I was sitting in a packed and darkened room, sharing a bottle of vodka with a couple of other men, when Pretos instructed me to 'suck the chain'. It was baffling to me at first.

"What do you mean?" I asked. "I don't understand."

In explanation, he laughed and pointed to the row of middle-aged men, sitting on sofas around the room. My insides liquified as the penny dropped. 'Suck the chain' was the stomach-churning phrase he, and others, used to refer to a girl performing oral sex on all the men present. One by one, along the chain, until everyone was satisfied. I dragged in a breath. My lungs felt as though they were shrinking. I could not do this. I could not. I looked at the faces leering back at me; all adults, some old enough to be my father. Some had long beards. Some had body odour. Some had dentures. Every bone in my body screamed out in protest against this.

I cannot do it… I cannot do it… I cannot do it…

But neither could I refuse.

"Good girl," Pretos smiled afterwards. "See? Fun game, isn't it?"

"Fun," I repeated, my revulsion spreading, like a rash, over my whole body.

Pretos himself often insisted on me removing my shoes and socks when I was alone with him. Sometimes, I was made to take my shoes and socks off in his car. Other times, it was at the parties. I learned that he had a bizarre foot fetish and he liked to see girls with bare feet so he could arouse himself. I had never even heard of a foot fetish until then, and it was as comical as it was disgusting to me, aged 15. I'd cringe inwardly as I rolled my socks off to reveal my bare feet, my whole body tensing like steel in anticipation for what was coming next.

"Paint your nails," he told me. "I like them like that. Nice colours."

I didn't like any of it, though I said nothing. But neither did I see it for what it was; grubby, deviant, grotesque paedophilia. I was too far gone for that; too frightened to speak up for myself, and also too immature and naive. I just saw it as part of the deal. And I was terrified of what might happen if I disobeyed; the threat was always there, that they would target my parents and my family home again. I dreaded a repetition of those phone calls, where they had abused my mum and threatened to hurt her. And I only had to hesitate or pull a face when I was told to do something, and I'd get a slap across the cheek. Other times, they stamped on me and left the imprints of their trainers on my back or stomach. They were painful, but at least I could hide those easily enough from my parents, under my clothes. But many nights, I went home with a black eye or a bruise on my cheek and I had to fabricate yet another fantastical story about yet another mugging.

"You're in with the wrong crowd," Mum would say, dabbing my injuries with antiseptic cream. "I don't know what's happened to you. I really don't. Good to bad. And nothing in between."

Showing weakness in front of the gang members, crying or pleading, just made them worse. I quickly learned there was no sympathy here, no basic humanity at all. It was better to act tough, and unconcerned, and hope the hard shell I pretended to have would one day grow for real around me as protection. I found myself laughing when I was faced with truly barbaric situations, not because they were remotely funny, but because it was the safest way to react.

I was worried too, that if I refused to cooperate, my supply of drugs and alcohol would dry up, and I might not be able to manage without them. Worse, I might be forced to make back payments for everything I'd consumed so far. I had no idea of the cost of drugs, but I knew without a doubt it would come to a lot more than my weekly pocket money, which, more often than not, was rescinded due to my behaviour.

And so, I couldn't and wouldn't walk away. I was trapped, ensnared, just as surely as if I had fallen into a dark tangle of barbed wire, and the more I tried to escape, the more my skin snagged and tore and bled. It was better just to stay still and accept what came my way.

When we weren't at parties, we were herded into cars, driving between the snooker hall and the taxi office, parking behind the Jet petrol station or near to the railway station. Some nights, we'd meet up at 'the hotspot' which was our nickname for a bridge linking two sections of the canal. Often, we'd be taken further afield. Some evenings, we went to the water treatment plant, or up to the reservoir, or to Scammonden Dam. Quiet and deserted, these were places where the men knew we wouldn't be disturbed, and spots where they knew we'd be too frightened to be dumped out in the cold and left behind. Taking us there was a perfect way of getting us to do exactly as we were told.

"You want to walk five miles home, in the pitch black?" Pretos would laugh. "Thought not. Do as I say then."

Up at the reservoir, we might be chatting and laughing quite normally, passing around a bottle of Jack Daniels or a cannabis joint. But then Pretos would suddenly turn and hiss:

"How do you think you're going to get home, then? What are you going to do to persuade me to drive you back?"

The car would fall silent, the drink suddenly sour in our mouths. Once, I made the mistake of replying:

"My dad will come and collect me."

There was a frisson of nervous tension across the back seat. And then Glen grabbed my hair and gave me a stinging slap across the face.

"You silly little bitch," he spat. "Do as you are told."

There was no way out. Each time we arrived at a remote location, and the engine died, my stomach plunged. The fear was electrifying. I knew what I had to do to get home. I had to do as I was told, without question, without hesitation. And sometimes, if Pretos decided I was less enthusiastic or less prompt than he'd like, he'd whip out a small knife from his back pocket and hold it to my throat whilst I performed oral sex. The first time he did it, I thought he was going to stab me. I began mentally saying my goodbyes, convinced I would never see my parents again.

"See this," he grinned, turning the blade so that it glinted in the light. "You take notice, you little slut."

I needed no more instruction. Yet he never cut me, I never had so much as a graze. The knife was just for show, just for laughs, like most things he did. But the cold, unyielding blade against my skin was reminder enough that he was in charge and always would be. He held my life in his hands.

Other times, if Pretos felt I'd been especially good, he would hand me a £10 note, or he'd buy me a bag of doner meat, as reward for my 'work'. As my wages. There was no joy in earning that kind of payment. The doner meat was dry and tough and scraped my throat. But I kept that thought to myself.

"Thanks," I'd say, tucking the money into my jeans. "Appreciate it."

Late one night, on the way back from the reservoir, Pretos suddenly pulled on the brakes and, without explanation, dumped me out of the car, and into the road, for no reason at all. He had earlier ordered me to remove my footwear so that he could perform a sex act, and I was barefooted.

"What?" I gasped, as he drove off into the distance. "What did I do?"

I had no idea why he had singled me out like that. And probably, neither did he. It was just for entertainment, for sport, to liven up his evening. Alone in the dark, I stumbled to the nearest bus stop, despite having no money, no shoes and socks on, and no coat. It didn't even occur to me how strange I must have looked. I was past caring what other people thought of me or what dangerous situations I kept falling into. I waited at the bus stop, knowing it was probably pointless without the fare; cold, miserable and afraid.

One of the other girls had thankfully persuaded another man from the gang to come and pick me up, and eventually, I saw a car slowing down as it came towards me. I was so grateful as I clambered into the passenger seat and yet of course the favour came with strings attached, and I had to do exactly as he said in exchange for a lift home.

"No problem," I said.

But again, the sheer wrongness of it was lost on me. I had no appreciation of the bigger picture, because I was too busy focussing on the smaller yet crucial details. I was swamped simply with the business of everyday survival.

That night, I was just thankful to be home, worrying about how I'd find my shoes and my coat and wondering whether I could get them back before Mum noticed they were missing.

'Please let me have my stuff back,' I texted Pretos. 'I need my coat and shoes. Please.'

When he handed them back to me, the following day, I threw my arms around him. And so, in my topsy-turvy world, I was overcome with gratitude towards him, thanking him even after he had dumped me in the middle of the countryside on my own and in bare feet. He had an uncanny knack of making me believe that I was always in the wrong.

"All is forgiven," he told me indulgently. "You know you're my special girl."

We sometimes drove to a sailing club in the evenings, and always parked on the same sandy patch at the edge of the water. It was deserted at night, and we had the place to ourselves. When I got out of the car, either to perform a sex act or to smoke a joint with one of the men, I was reminded, with excruciating poignancy, of my holidays in Kerry and our trips to the beach with my cousins. Those days felt so far away, right now. In Ireland, I loved the feeling of soft sand beneath my feet and in between my toes. But now, a sandy floor under my bare feet felt unsafe, as though I might sink right through it and never get out again.

* * * *

As I try to formulate a rigid timeline of my teenage years, my memories of the parties are hazy and fuzzy, partly because I was often so drunk or drugged up, and partly too because I blocked out much of what happened because it was so horribly raw.

And in addition, there was not much to distinguish one party from the next. They all seemed to blur and bleed into one; a different house, a different man, a different drug. Same abuse. The parties were nondescript and generic and yet mind-blowing. I couldn't work out which statement was correct.

Occasionally, something out of the ordinary might happen, something so shocking and so sadistic that it was wedged obstinately in my mind, despite my best efforts to wipe it. But in the main, my memories floated and bobbed, like disjointed and displaced vignettes of horror. I didn't know where or when the atrocities had happened. I certainly did not know why. I only knew, without doubt, that they had.

I do remember, in the early days at the parties, being wrong-footed and dejected by Glen's behaviour. He watched and cheered the sex acts along with all the others, as though he was enjoying a raucous game show on telly. I tried not to let myself dwell on the fact that he was supposed to be my boyfriend, that he had once, very sweetly, taken my hand in his and hooked my hair behind my ear. That I had, in my naivety, hoped that he would love me and look after me. I remembered writing our initials, inside a love heart, on the underside of the slide in the park. How foolish I had been. I wanted to flash back and shake my 14-year-old self, warn her off, before it got too late. For now, without doubt, it was too late.

Often, the sex acts were filmed and passed around, so that the horror and humiliation of the assault dragged on, into eternity, and the threat that they could be shared – with our parents or with our peers or our teachers – hovered over us like a dark and heavy cloud. We didn't understand that the gang wouldn't have dared share the videos with adults, because it was them, and not us, who would have been culpable.

It was one of my worst fears that they might send clips of the films to my parents; I would often wake up in the early hours in a cold, panicky sweat, worrying about it. The irony was that it would have been the best thing possible to happen. Those films were my currency for change; not theirs. The whole gang would have been arrested and vilified if the videos had ever been exposed and that would have spelled the end of the abuse. But at 15, I had no idea how the world worked, and the men all knew that. They played on my innocence and on my fear, and whilst the videos were entertainment for them, they were also another form of control.

Once, one of the girls was forced to have sex with an elderly man who walked with a stick. I wasn't at that particular party, but I saw the footage afterwards and it was like a bear-pit with men jumping up and down and hollering in excitement. She was in the middle of it all, a broken centrepiece, her face pitifully pale, her eyes empty and lost. And though I was despairing and disgusted at the scene, I did no more than raise my eyebrows and snigger. For the bigger part of me was so grateful that it was her, and not me. I handed back the phone, when the clip was finished, with a broad smile.

"Wow," I said. "What a film."

At another party, one of the girls was given a bottle of vodka and after she had taken a mouthful, she was told it was urine. One of the gang members had peed into the bottle, as a sick joke.

"And she actually drank it!" they yelled, guffawing with laughter. "So funny!"

"Yes," I agreed, forcing a smile. "Hilarious."

We were treated worse than lab rats; existing only to provide the gang with sex and entertainment and excruciating anecdotes which they could later share and dissect amongst themselves. I found their sense of humour very odd. I found their total absence of humanity even odder.

One night, as we drove around Huddersfield, one of the girls was made to simulate sex with the car gear stick. Her humiliation, as I watched on, was toe-curling. I wanted to cover my eyes; it was too awful to witness. But none of us dared to speak out, we laughed along, and pretended it was funny, because that was the easiest way. That was the safest way.

On another night, I had swallowed a cocktail of booze and drugs, and I was violently sick afterwards. I staggered outside, into the night air, with absolutely no idea of where I was going or even of who I was. I floundered through the streets in a purgatorial haze, desperately in need of help, knowing there was none out there. Flooded with despair, I clung to a lamppost to steady myself.

"Dad," I whispered feebly. "I need you."

I stumbled on a little further, tempted just to lie down, in the road, and wait for fate to take its course. Could that be a way out for me?

"Dad," I mumbled again.

Then, to my amazement, through the darkness and the quiet of the sleepy streets, I heard the familiar noise of his truck. It had a unique sound; a noisy, grumbly sort of engine. At first, I thought it was a hallucination, a cruel trick of my subconscious. When I saw the truck, taking physical shape before me and slowing down at the side of the road, I burst into tears of relief.

"Oh, love, what's happened to you?" Dad gasped.

He jumped out of his seat and ran around to lift me into the passenger side. I was so overwhelmed, so grateful, so exhausted, that I couldn't even speak. Besides, I didn't know where to start. What had happened to me? I didn't even know.

"You're covered in sick," Dad said. "And look at all those scratches on your cheek!

"Your mum and me have been looking everywhere for you. It's so late. I've been driving around for ages. I'm so glad I've got you. So glad you're safe.

"What's going on, pet? Please tell me what's wrong?"

The tears flowed, dripping onto my hands, mixing with the splatter of vomit on my shirt. I wanted so much to tell him. But I stayed silent. My own heart was broken, and I knew how painful that felt. I couldn't bring myself to break his too.

"Thanks," I mumbled eventually. "Thanks for picking me up."

It became a regular thing; Dad would drive round the streets looking for me when I was late home. He did laps of familiar routes, again and again, hoping to catch sight of me. There was never any recrimination or punishment from him when he finally found me. He didn't understand what was going on. But he did what he could, which was to get me home safe and sound.

Mum, on the other hand, wanted information and details, as mothers do. She demanded answers. She needed to know where I was, why I had bruises, why I was drunk, why I'd lost my mobile phone. It all added to her conviction that I was hanging around with a bunch of older girls and that they were leading me astray, plying me with alcohol and encouraging me to stay out late.

"It's that new crowd," she declared, over and over again.

If only it had been that simple.

* * * *

As the self-appointed MC at the parties, Pretos took charge of pairing off each girl with a man or a group of men. I saw money changing hands on many occasions, but I presumed this was to pay for alcohol and drugs and whatever else. Now, as an adult, I wonder whether the money was meant for something more.

"Get 'em while they're young," Pretos liked to say, rubbing his hands together, almost salivating as he inspected our bare feet. "They need breaking in."

It was as though he was sizing up a line of animals at a cattle market, choosing the one he fancied most, selecting the throat he would most like to slit.

At many of the parties, Pretos organised a 'dare' game where he'd dare us to have sex, in front of everyone. Or he'd dare us to insert items internally. Or he'd dare us to strip naked and parade around the house.

"I dare…" he'd say, and in that moment, I would feel my heartbeat actually pause and stutter, in blind panic.

Once, I was made to insert a bottle, with a room full of adult men staring at me, cheering and screaming in a gladiatorial manner as the frivolities got underway. I had to bite back on the discomfort and humiliation and do as I was told. Other times, I had to let men masturbate over me, or I was forced to have sex or oral sex.

The concept of the game was fatally flawed because there was no other option available to us. Pretos was the only one allowed to make the dare. And it wasn't a dare. It was an order. It was rape. The game was simply a way of adding another dimension to their perversions. The word 'game' like the word 'party' was tarnished and ruined for me now. They were pillaging my vocabulary, along with my peace of mind, along with my childhood.

Even though I knew it would end badly for me, I often tried, at parties, to put off the inevitable in some way or another. It was a survival instinct and I just couldn't help myself.

"I don't feel well today," I'd say. "I might be coming down with something."

Or:

"I'm in my school uniform. I might get into trouble."

Or:

"Can't we just talk? I'd like to talk to you. Really, I would."

But it failed every time. The response was as clear as it was cruel:

"I haven't spent all this money on Bacardi and Chickers to talk to you, you stupid little slag. Do as you're told or you'll get battered."

Some of the men didn't speak English and so as soon as I started talking, they would shut me up with a smack across the face. What I dreaded most was a complaint making its way back to Pretos, because he hated to hear a bad review. I was so frightened of making him mad.

There were rarely any condoms used at the parties, and occasionally, the men would use plastic bags – grabbed from a kitchen drawer – instead. Once I saw them empty out a carrier bag, shaking shopping onto the floor, so that it could be used as make-shift contraception. The general impression was always that the bags were for their protection, and not ours. I didn't even think about the hygiene aspect, less still about pregnancy or sexually transmitted diseases. Of all my worries, and I had many, picking up a disease was not amongst them. In many ways, I was so pitifully naïve and gullible. In other ways, I was world-weary and aged before my time.

As I settled into playing truant again at my new school with Pretos meeting me outside the gates, he would sometimes bring other men, total strangers, along with him.

One afternoon, he texted to tell me to leave my lesson, immediately. I made an excuse to the bemused teacher about needing the loo and then I walked straight out of the main entrance doors. Pretos was waiting, with two strange men in the car. He drove me to a quiet side street, ordered me out of the car, and nodded towards one of the men. Then he said:

"Go and have sex with him."

The man got out too and I stared at him, as helpless as I was horrified. I didn't want to do this, I had no idea who he was, but I knew I could not say no.

I had sex with him up against the wall, in full view of the occupants of the car, and anyone else driving past. Afterwards, I got back in the Micra, straightening my school tie and smoothing down my skirt. Pretos and his friends laughed all the way through the journey back to school, as though taking me out for an 'express rape' was the most hilarious thing they'd ever done.

I slipped back through the doors and walked into the same lesson I had left. I sank heavily into my chair, and the teacher made a sarcastic comment about the length of time I'd spent in the toilet.

"Yeah, sorry, Miss," I replied stonily.

I didn't care about any punishment she might hand out. Nothing could ever compare to what I had just been through.

Another time, I was again ordered to leave school early, and there were three men in the car when Pretos collected me. He parked up near to the snooker hall and said:

"Right, we've got a few little jobs for you, Tina."

I was ordered to perform group sex acts, in broad daylight, in the car, whilst one of the men filmed it all. Panic scissored through me. I felt myself gagging just at the thought of it.

"Come on, baby," one of the men said, unzipping his jeans, and I knew there was no way out. But part way through, as I screwed my eyes shut, I felt myself floating, up off the seat and out of the car window, and into the grey drizzle of the afternoon. As I glided down the street, a breeze caught my ponytail, and I felt the light rain settling on my skin. It was blissful, up here in the air, away from the men.

"Tina!"

I snapped back to reality with Pretos glaring at me.

"Finish the job!"

I stared at him, disorientated to find myself back in the car, half-dressed, with strange men ogling me.

"I need the toilet," I stuttered. "I'm sorry, I really need some air. I can't do it."

Retching, I pushed past one of the men and fell out of the car door. I ran into the snooker hall, intending to use the toilet there, wondering whether I dare summon enough courage to keep on running. And running. As far away as I could.

But on the stairs inside the hall, I felt a damp hand on my shoulder and sharp nails digging into my skin.

"You're going nowhere," Pretos growled. "Get back in the car."

He dragged me backwards down the stairs and along the street as though I was a bag of rubbish. The other men had gone.

Once we were in the car, just me and him, he drove like a madman up to the reservoir. My heart was slamming against my ribs. I knew what was coming, and the anticipation was unbearable. I just wanted it to be over.

At the reservoir, Pretos subjected me to a brutal and violent rape. I might just as well have been pitchforked into hell. I felt absolutely wretched. Every bone in my body sobbed, and afterwards, as I clasped my head in my hands, he said: "That's because you showed me up in front of my boys."

He drove me back to school, dropping me at the gates, as though perhaps I'd just been out for a dental check-up or an eye test.

It was not lost on me, as I walked unsteadily down the corridor, that I had started playing truant to avoid the bullies who treated me like a piece of meat and I had walked straight into the dark and evil bowels of a child sex ring.

8

In it Together

As time passed, and the gang grew larger and more wide-spread, more and more girls were recruited. There were splinter groups, and so some men I saw daily, others only occasionally. Certain men, I saw just once. In our section, Pretos was still most definitely in charge. He continued to encourage me to bring along friends from school or from my neighbourhood. I was under pressure to deliver.

Since moving schools, I saw much less of my old pals, even though we all lived in the same area. There was an awkward distance between us. The kudos I believed I'd earned by hanging around with the men had mutated into something ugly and undesirable. Now, instead of being bullied for my weight, I was singled out and targeted because I was sleeping with Asian men. I had lost the 'fat' label, in exchange for 'slag' or 'slut'. I had no friends at my new school and I was losing touch with my old mates. Inevitably, I was being pushed further and further into the grasp of the gang. Nobody else wanted me. Nobody else understood.

At first, the girls all got along well together. We were all of a similar age, background, and social demographic. I had a couple of close friends within the structure of the gang. I met one girl, named Clare, at a party. I felt sorry for her because one of the gang members had thrown her outside on the street in the dark, and she was throwing up into the gutter. I followed her out to hold her hair back and offer her a glass of water, and we got chatting. Afterwards, with so much in common, we became best pals. It didn't change what was happening to us, but it did help that we weren't going through it all alone. It was such a comfort to know that I wasn't completely on my own and that someone else understood my dilemma and my torment.

"I was bullied at school, that's why I started skipping lessons," Clare confessed. "I got in with the gang and I thought they were great, they bought me takeaways and loads of vodka and cigs. I thought they were my mates.

"Then they started making me do stuff I didn't like, and they rang my mum and shouted abuse at her. I have to do as they say. I'm worried what they'll do to me otherwise. My big fear is that they'll hurt my family."

My jaw dropped. It was a carbon copy of my own situation. I was stunned by the similarities. Yet, as a child, I was only amazed by the coincidence, I did not see the deliberate pattern, the orchestrated grooming, the systematic targeting and brainwashing of young and vulnerable girls.

"I'm the same," I told her. "Bullied, skipped school, met Pretos at the bus station. Now I'm stuck with him."

It was a desperate and essentially hopeless situation. But like all kids, we were resilient and forward-looking, and we bounced off each other, making light of the trauma, finding humour in the grotesque. Even after a really horrible evening, it took just one text from Clare to make me smile again:

'Eww! See what I had to do? He looked like Frankenstein!'

'Mine was worse. Breath smelled like dog poo.'

We exchanged notes on the men who abused us, like most kids swap complaints about homework. The horrific became routine. The extraordinary almost became boring. Slowly, we were becoming desensitised to the abuse. We would never consent to it, but we were beginning to accept there was nothing we could do about it. And having friends, and allies, and someone just to roll my eyes at, really meant the world to me. Clare was on my side.

'I had those new pills last night. Made me sick. Avoid if u can!'

'Thanks hun. Watch out. Pretos is in foul mood. U take care.'

One night, at a party, we were both paired up with men we knew, and loathed. A few swigs of vodka did nothing to dampen down my dismay and I was dreading what was coming next.

"I need the loo," Clare announced, and she tilted her chin, almost imperceptibly, in my direction.

A couple of minutes later, I excused myself too.

"Won't be a minute," I promised.

I tapped on the bathroom door and Clare let me in.

"What do you think?" she asked, nodding towards the window. "It's a flat roof outside. Easy."

There was an irresistible glint of mischief in her eyes.

"Go for it," I grinned, already locking the bathroom door

behind us. We opened the window and dropped silently onto a roof below. From there, we jumped easily onto a grassy bank. As we fell onto the wet grass, and rolled a little, I was overcome with a fit of giggles. Stifling my laughter, I clambered to my feet, and we ran down the street. I was reminded of those early days at high school; laughing as we ran away from the deputy head teacher. Now, as then, I was high on life.

"We're in so much trouble," I gasped, as I stopped to catch my breath. "But I would do it all again."

We sent Pretos a jumbled text that one of us was ill and the other had taken her home. We knew it would make no difference. We'd be punished, the next day, and severely too. But somehow, knowing we were in it together just made it all worth it. Just that once, it felt so good to take control.

'Still got grass in my shoes,' Clare texted later.

'Me 2,' I replied. 'Loved it.'

I am unsure whether it was a calculated decision, but when Pretos saw us forming friendships and bonding, he swiftly put a stop to it. Perhaps he was worried that, strength in numbers, we would form an alliance and go to the police or confide in our parents. But I think he was too arrogant to even think about getting caught. More likely, he had a cruel, vicious streak and he just did not like to see us smile. He did not want us to have friends, he did not like us to have any relationships which extended outside the gang, because that lessened our dependency on him. He wanted total control.

At the parties, he began pitting us against one other, encouraging us to shame and degrade each other. Some girls were forced to perform sex acts on each other. Other times, he made one of us choose the girl in his 'dare' game, so that it was our decision, our fault, that she was subsequently raped. There were arguments and fights and our friendships, already fragile, splintered and shattered like smashed glass. I dreaded each time my phone bleeped with a message from one of my pals.

'Thanks for nothing Tina. Why choose me?'

'U r next.'

'Never liked u anyway bitch.'

One day, I was at a house belonging to one of the gang, along with a girl pal. I was sent upstairs with a man, and when I came back down, I saw her on the sofa, clearly unconscious, with her top pulled up and her jeans pulled down. There was a man on top of her. I started to object, but the words stuck in my throat and drizzled into silence. I wasn't even sure whether she was still alive, and she was definitely in no fit state to know what was happening to her. I stood at the door, caught in two minds, wanting to step in, but too scared to do it. Uncertainty flickered within me like a stuttering candle.

"Is she okay?" I asked nervously, almost inaudibly.

There was no response. I stared, panic rising. Should I call the police? Suddenly, the man realised he was being watched. He stood up and marched over, before shoving me roughly against the wall. My feet left the floor, and my throat was squeezed. With one hand around my neck, he shoved the other hand down the front of my pants. He pushed his face up close to mine so that a fine spray of foul-smelling spittle landed on my cheeks.

"Get out," he hissed. "Now!"

I had no option but to leave her there and run. I felt torn in two, even as I reached the safety of home. It seemed cowardly and wrong to leave her there to be raped, but I had no choice. It was survival of the fittest, each out for themselves.

'Sorry' I texted her later. 'I wanted 2 help. He made me leave. '

But in her reply she was understandably furious and upset. And so that was another friendship ruined. Another ally gone. Alone, isolated and vulnerable, it was me versus the gang, me versus the rest of the world, and the pain hurt so much more.

Our frightened little cluster of teenage girls walked around Huddersfield, hiding the same secrets, cradling the same sorrows. It was like being part of a cult. We might as well have had chains around our hands and feet, dragging us back, always, to the gang. There was no escape. I felt dirty, broken and lost. At 15 years of age, I did not see a way out. I did not see a way forward with my life.

It was not unusual, at the parties, for one of the girls to overdose, accidentally or not, on booze or drugs or, more frequently, a mix of the two. It was more common still for one of us to take a beating. At different times, we each found ourselves in hospital, or at the doctors, or at the family planning clinic. We missed school, we withdrew from family life, we failed exams, we argued with our parents, we ran away from home. We existed only on the periphery, mere ghosts of our former selves, harrowing reminders of the children we once were. And yet, nobody joined the dots. Not the teachers, or the social workers, or the police, or the nurses and doctors at the family planning clinics. Nobody stopped to ask why all these girls were 'in with the wrong crowd' and why they had all 'gone off the rails'.

There was a toxic cord binding us all together. But nobody spotted it. Nobody ever asked why.

* * * *

Throughout 2006, and into 2007, my whole life revolved around the gang. I learned to compartmentalise the abuse, and package it away, more and more effectively as time went on. On the one hand, I was an errant teenager, driving my parents mad with my love of partying and under-age drinking, and probably they believed I was not untypical of many girls my age.

Yet the dark underbelly of my parallel existence; the gang, the grooming and the sexual abuse, served as a hidden and sinister reminder that all was not as it seemed. It was like a rotten fruit; deceivingly healthy on the surface, but underneath the skin was a stinky, pulpy mess.

By now, we were travelling further afield in the evenings; a combination perhaps of me caring less and less about the trouble I was in at home and the gang's desire to take us out of Huddersfield and away from our families and the familiarity of home surroundings.

One night, on the instructions of Pretos, I was driven to a hotel in Bradford with three men. I was forced to have sex with them all, in a hotel room, and afterwards, in the early hours, they gathered their phones and wallets and buttoned up their coats, ready to leave.

"What about me?" I asked frantically. "Will you take me back to Huddersfield?"

One of the men laughed as if I'd asked him to take me to the moon.

"You can make your own way," he sniggered, turning his back.

"But I can't get home!" I objected. "You can't leave me here in the middle of the night. Please!"

I followed them down the corridors like a lost kitten, pleading with them to help me get home.

"You drove me here," I dared to point out. "Why won't you drive me back?"

In the hotel foyer, one of the men turned on me, his fist raised in the air, ready to thump me.

"Shut up!" he yelled. "Just shut the fuck up!"

The hotel receptionist, who had been watching, came out from behind his desk with his hands outstretched before him in a placatory gesture.

"She's just a child!" he said nervously. "Please don't hurt her!"

He exchanged words briefly with the men, before they marched me outside, with them, and away from the suspicion of the hotel staff. I peered back over my shoulder, hoping against hope that the receptionist might follow and offer to help me. But there was no sign of him. I wondered in frustration why he had stepped in during the row yet didn't seem to think it was strange for a young teenager to share a hotel room with three angry adults. We had different skin colours. We were clearly not related. It was obvious just by looking at us that I was there under duress. But perhaps he was too scared. Perhaps, as on so many occasions before, people saw what was going on but simply didn't want to get involved. They had enough problems of their own.

"Please take me home," I said again.

But once we had walked further up the pavement, right away from the hotel, the men shoved me aside, got into their car, and drove away. I was left there all alone. It was late, around 1am, and I was cold and frightened, and in a strange town. I wanted so much to call my parents; more than anything I longed to hear the throaty sound of Dad's truck chugging up the street. But I knew they'd both be in bed, they had work in just a few hours, and I couldn't bring myself to disturb them. Besides, I'd then have to conjure up a reasonable explanation for how I'd ended up in Bradford in the middle of the night, over half-an-hour's drive from home. Shivering, and hopping from one foot to the other, I flagged down a passing taxi. I didn't have a penny on me, but I knew better than to tell the driver that.

"Huddersfield, please," I said.

On the journey home, I tapped my hands together nervously, wishing it all could be over. As we arrived at the bottom of our street, parking a few doors from my home so as not to alert my parents, I handed the driver my phone, as surety.

"Just wait five minutes," I pleaded. "I'll be back with the fare."

Creeping inside, past Vicky, who was sleeping on the mat, I saw to my relief that Dad's keys were hanging on the usual hook, and with them a tiny safe key. I tip-toed down to the basement, where, behind the washing-machine, he had a safe. There wasn't a great deal in there; usually just a few hundred pounds from building jobs, but I knew there'd be enough to cover the taxi fare. I ran outside to pay the driver and collect my phone, before creeping back in and up the stairs. Collapsing into bed, I felt overwhelming relief. In my child's mind, the rapes were overshadowed by my struggle to get home. The abuse was becoming so common-place to me that I accepted it as part of my daily routine and I had reached a point where being stranded in a strange town was as much, or more of, a worry than a brutal sexual attack.

One of Pretos' favourite haunts was Saddleworth Moor. It was around half-an-hour out of town, and I hated going there. I knew, as everyone did, that this was where Ian Brady and Myra Hindley had buried their victims, and the name itself evoked feelings of utter horror in me. And our first trip up there was every bit as bleak and forbidding as I'd imagined. Out of the window, I gazed upon swathe upon swathe of desolate moorland. We were miles from civilisation, miles from home.

"Nobody will hear you scream up here," Pretos sniggered.

His laughter was laced with menace as he killed the engine and lit up a spliff. I laughed along nervously, eyeing the steering wheel lock which he kept in the footwell. I had never seen him use it to secure his car, but he had threatened me and the other girls with it on many occasions. I'd also seen baseball bats and lumps of wood in his car boot. And of course, I knew he had a knife. Out here, in the middle of nowhere, thinking of the poor children whose remains had been buried somewhere in the gloom, my imagination ran riot. I felt as though Pretos was capable of anything. He nodded to the two men either side of me on the back seat, and I knew what I had to do.

"You wouldn't want to get left behind, would you?" he said. "Not in the dark, not on the moors. Surely not?"

And that was all it needed. I had heard, from the others, that he had thrown one girl out of the car and left her overnight on Saddleworth Moor. I knew he wouldn't think twice about doing the same to me. He was perfectly capable of such evil and would probably quite enjoy it. The men were already unbuckling their belts and unzipping their jeans, and, as I closed my eyes, I tried to focus on my Groovy Chick bed, my Rosie doll, my soft grey cat, snoring on the sofa.

"It will soon be over," I told myself. "You will soon be home."

And even after I had done everything asked of me, every last nauseating, loathsome detail, Pretos strung me along just that little bit more. He tutted and hummed and pretended to consider whether I was worthy of a lift home.

"Well, let me see," he deliberated, his voice cold and cruel.

I cried tears of relief when he eventually agreed to drive me back.

"Thank you," I said, hastily trying to wipe my eyes.

Once again, he had that knack of making me feel grateful to him for being wicked towards me.

On another outing, Pretos took us to Manchester. A couple of other cars, packed with the gang and with other girls, arranged to meet us there. The motorway drive was hair-raising, as he popped pills and threw his hands up in the air, off the steering wheel, at speeds of over 70mph. Part of me was petrified, but a bigger part of me was thrilled, and I was keen to embrace the risk. Like any teenager, I had a strong sense of invincibility, and the drink and drugs helped to dull any nagging sense of danger. We parked on a back street behind the famous curry mile in Rusholme, and there was a buzz of excitement rippling through our group as we ordered takeaway kebabs and samosas. To a passer-by, we must have looked like we were having a ball, giggling and eating our food as we walked down the bustling and brightly lit streets. We were an unusual group, middle-aged Asian men and young white teenage girls. But there were no outward signs of any tension and again, nobody stopped to ask who we were.

"Who ate all the samosas?" Pretos exclaimed. "Greedy cows!"

It was good-natured teasing. Yet even as I laughed, deep in the pit of my stomach, was the sickly knowledge that soon I would be called upon to pay for this fun. I struggled to swallow the last of my kebab as I thought about the long journey home, past the dark moors at Saddleworth.

On our way out of Manchester, we saw flashing lights behind us. Pretos was pulled over by police officers who reprimanded him, as I understood it, for having too many passengers in his car.

"Step out please," said an officer, and Pretos did as he said.

Another officer peered through the car window at us, and I wondered whether he might also question what Pretos was doing with 15-year-old girls on the back seat. But after a short chat at the side of the road, the police car drove away and I had no idea what punishment, if any, he received. It added to my feeling of invincibility and also to the belief that perhaps Pretos and his associates were doing nothing wrong. I was the guilty one. Not them. It was reinforced, time after time.

One Saturday, Pretos announced we were off to Blackpool. The gang had hired or borrowed a minibus from the taxi rank, and we all crammed in together. Again, it was so much fun, squashed up with the other girls, sharing vodka, trying on each other's lipsticks, admiring each other's trainers. Yet knowing with cold certainty that we would all, me included, readily offer each other up to be gang raped, to save ourselves. The camaraderie, the friendship, was so thin and brittle that I could almost hear it straining and fraying above the music, always ready to snap.

In Blackpool, the gang appeared to have unlimited funds available. I never questioned where the money came from. I didn't really want to know and besides, it was none of my business. We had plenty of cash to squander in the arcades, to buy ice-creams and candyfloss, to pay for roller-coaster rides. It was a rare sunny day, and the Blackpool pavements were teeming with people keen to make the most of the weather. We could have been holidaymakers. Day trippers. It could all just have been innocent amusement.

"Having a good time, babe?" Glen asked, pinching some of my candyfloss.

I nodded and smiled. But the unease sat in my stomach, solid like a brick. As the day went on, it grew larger and larger, expanding until it filled my thorax, compressing my lungs, making it painful for me to take in a breath. When we got back in the minibus, ready to go home, Pretos smiled thinly and said:

"Well, you owe me now, girls. You owe us all. Big time."

9

In a Mess

In the months which followed the trips to Blackpool and Manchester, and the countless nights when I was late home, or I came in drunk or drugged or covered with bruises and vomit, my parents worried more and more, until the issue of my behaviour was dominating our family life.

"This isn't just about you hanging around with the wrong crowd," Mum said. "There's more to this. I want to know the truth, Christina. What's going on?"

I met every one of her well-meaning questions with a stony glare or a sarcastic roll of the eyes.

"Well, that's it, then," she'd say. "You're getting no pocket money this week. And I'm confiscating your phone."

But of course that meant nothing to me. I knew Pretos had money and phones and drugs, just waiting for me.

"That's fine, Mum," I'd say. "Whatever."

She did her best to find out what I was up to. She insisted on taking me to the GP for drug tests. They later came back with a positive result for cannabis and my parents gave me a strict talking to.

"You need to steer clear of drugs," Dad said seriously. "I

know you might think that cannabis is harmless, but it's not. You need to think about your schoolwork."

I knew I was letting them down and in my own way, I was remorseful. But still my terror of the gang overruled any feelings of regret I had for my parents.

"Won't do it again, Dad," I lied.

They didn't believe me, quite rightly, and Mum conducted a search of my bedroom, forensically checking all my drawers and cupboards, even pulling the mattress off my bed. She eventually found a small forgotten bag of M-kat in my sock drawer. M-kat was a step up, in my mind, from ecstasy pills, because it was snorted and not swallowed. It made me feel cool and grown up. Far from being worried about Mum's reaction, I saw it as something of a status symbol.

"Where on earth are you getting these drugs from?" she asked in despair. "I need to know. I'm going to speak to your teachers too."

My education was spiralling downwards faster than ever before. Up to Year Eight, I'd never had an unauthorised absence from school. By Year Nine, I'd missed 55 days and there were countless unrecorded too. Year 10 was even worse. I was hardly ever there. But my teachers had no answers for Mum. They were at a loss, just as she was.

As a last resort, when I was late home one night, my parents called the police. Dad was already out, driving round Huddersfield searching for me, and Mum was waiting at the house for the police to show up. By the time I finally got home, worse for wear, there were two officers waiting in the living room. Mum was giving them a detailed account of my downfall.

"She's typical of a lot of teenagers," sighed the officer. "They do tend to go off the rails around this age, I'm afraid."

And that was it. That was as good as it got. Mum called them time after time, but they were never able to offer any constructive advice or support. The burden weighed heavy on her and my dad, yet they were forced to carry it alone. And even though I could see them struggling under the strain, my own hardship was greater, and so I could not reach out to them.

"I feel like I'm losing you, pet," Dad said sadly.

I nodded miserably. I felt as though I was losing myself.

As well as marking me with bruises, the men in the gang also liked to leave love bites on my body and neck, as a sign of ownership. There were times when I had a line of bites, right round my neck, which was a source of great amusement to Pretos and his mates. In school, I was teased and taunted for them; the other kids had seen Pretos at the school gates and knew that I was hanging around with a group of Asian men. At home, I tried to hide them the best I could. I knew my parents would be mortified. But one morning, as I was coming out of the bathroom, Mum caught sight of my neck and gasped.

"Where did you get those?" she demanded.

The worry scudded across her face like a black shadow, and I felt a momentary stab of guilt. But I couldn't afford to dwell on that. Instead I shrugged, sullenly.

"Have you got a boyfriend?" she asked. "I need to know, Christina. You're only 15."

But as usual, I clammed up. I couldn't possibly begin to tell her the truth. I couldn't even tell myself the truth. The next day, she took me to see the GP.

"I'm really worried about her," Mum told the doctor. "I'd like her to have the contraceptive pill please."

It was an unexpected development for me; I hadn't even thought about the risks of pregnancy. From then, Mum made sure I took the pill religiously each morning, whilst lecturing me on the dangers of unprotected sex. She pleaded with me to tell her the identity of my boyfriend, but I said:

"I don't have a boyfriend."

The sad thing was, I was telling the truth.

Weeks later, after taking the pill each day, I noticed I was gaining weight. Immediately, I blamed my new medication, and I stopped taking it. Like most teenagers, my horizons were limited. I thought no further than the immediate future and for me, putting on a few pounds was a bigger problem than the risk of falling pregnant.

"I won't get pregnant," I yelled at Mum. "Stop interfering in my life. I'm not taking something that makes me fat and that's the end of it."

Mum and I argued about it, of course, back and forth like rapid gunfire, and it became just another issue on a long list of grievances we had with each other. The breakdown of my relationship with my parents felt like the least of my problems back then. It was a peripheral concern, juggling for space with all the other issues I had to put up with. But looking back, I can see how frightening and frustrating, and above all, how unspeakably sad, it must have been for them. I came from such a tight-knit family. Respectable. Normal.

My grandfather was a former police officer and local councillor. My parents were both hard working and law abiding; they were neither living in poverty nor were they particularly well off. We were typical, traditional, average, in every way.

Mum and I had once been so close; we shared a love of Disney and we'd curl up on the sofa at weekends to watch our favourite film, *Beauty and the Beast*. Mum was a fan of UB40 and she and I loved having a dance in the kitchen with her favourite CD blaring. As a little girl, I'd enjoyed so many days out at the beach or at the park with Mum and my aunty and cousins. We had a normal mother-daughter bond within the context of a wider, supportive family.

Yet at heart, I was a daddy's girl and always would be. My favourite times and recollections would always be those Saturday mornings helping out 'scotching', or the Sunday afternoons watching *Only Fools and Horses*. Dad's idea of rule-breaking was me sipping his Guinness with the dash of red Lucozade on top. He'd have been appalled if he knew just a small snippet of what was going on in the dark tangles of my other life.

Dad followed Gaelic football and was of course a passionate Kerry fan, which is where I got it from. We'd tune in the radio to pick up match commentary, cheering and hugging when results went our way. Our little unit, Mum, Dad and me, had once been compact, secure and happy.

But now, the foundations of my family were crumbling underfoot. The Disney films seemed ridiculously childish and inappropriate to me – there was, I knew from bitter experience, no such thing as a fairy-tale ending in real life. And I couldn't go out 'scotching' or drinking Lucozade with Dad. I felt like a fraud. I didn't feel as if I belonged anymore. I had let my parents down and I had lost my place in the family. I had sunk so low that there was no way back up for me.

In rows, I begged to be allowed to go to live in Ireland, with my cousins and aunts and uncles, and all of Dad's extended family. I saw it as a safe haven, a chance to escape the gangs, to simply vanish and never come back.

"No way," Mum said. "We can't send you over there to cause trouble for your aunts and uncles. We need you here where we can keep an eye on you. When you start being reasonable, we will definitely consider taking you over there for a holiday."

I felt like screaming in frustration. 'Here' was the crux of the problem. 'There' was the cure. In Ireland, there would be no trouble. Huddersfield was the issue, not me. My behaviour was geographically influenced.

"Remember how good I was when we went over to Kerry on holiday?" I reminded her. "You commented that I was like the old Christina. Remember?"

But Mum shook her head and Dad agreed with her.

"You have to get through this and it's our job to help you," he said. We can't just send you over to my family when you're behaving like this. You're our daughter. Not theirs."

At school, too, my behaviour had dropped another couple of notches. I no longer cared whether I was caught truanting. Sometimes, I'd get a text from Pretos part way through a lesson, and I'd just stand up and blatantly walk out. I didn't even explain myself to the teachers. I made no effort to even attempt my classwork and less still my homework. If a teacher tried to discipline me, I'd swear at the top of my voice and scoff at their punishments. I was always more interested in impressing the kids around me than addressing my own problems.

Once I had worked out that the worst consequence of my behaviour was a detention or a suspension, I felt strangely and wonderfully untouchable. Compared to the beatings and the threats I got from Pretos and the gang, my teachers were laughably impotent. During one detention, Pretos messaged me to say he was outside the school, and so I just got up and left, without any announcement. The other kids on detention told the teacher that I was being picked up outside by an Asian man. By now, they all knew about the gang, and I was ruthlessly teased. I had gone from bragging about my new privileges to being branded as unclean. I was more of an outsider now, ironically, than I had ever been in Year Seven, when I was targeted by the bullies over a few extra pounds. I had thought then that my worries were insurmountable. I realised now, as I scurried out of school and across the carpark to meet Pretos, how tragically mistaken I had been.

"There she is, look Miss," the other kids shouted, banging on the window at me.

But the detention teacher did nothing as I left the school gates. She didn't even try to stop me.

Another day, after I had been sent out of class for bad behaviour, a school support worker made me a cup of tea and asked me what was wrong. I stirred my tea and was furious to feel the tears pricking my eyes. I remembered a party, the previous weekend, where I had been forced to have sex with two men. I wasn't intending to say anything to the support worker. But then my mouth opened and seemed to work all of its own accord, and I heard myself mumbling:

"I have to do all kinds of bad stuff. I'm in a mess."

I couldn't form the words properly and I was shaking so much I had to put my cup down.

"What like?" she asked.

But I shook my head and blinked my tears away. Like a flower in the frost, I closed up, shutting out the outside world. But that one sentence was enough, or should have been enough, to raise serious concerns with her and the rest of the staff. Even so, to my knowledge, nothing more was done.

On a separate occasion, following another exclusion from class, I tried again, in a moment of weakness, to confide in an educational support worker. I told her that I, and other girls, were being badly treated by a gang in Huddersfield.

"I'm sick of it," I admitted. "Can't take much more."

But again, as far as I knew, nothing came of it. Wearily, I told myself I was a hopeless case. Shamefully, I reminded myself that this was all my fault. I certainly felt that way. And it explained why nobody wanted to listen.

Mum, meanwhile, continued to badger the police for help.

"Not much we can do unfortunately. It's not just the kids from the estates who go wrong," they told her. "This can happen to anyone. You really need to try and keep her at home. Be more vigilant."

She was at the end of her tether. But by now, she was beginning to suspect that I was mixed up in some way with older men. She understood without doubt that this was about far more than 'the wrong crowd' of older girls which she had believed for so long. She remembered our neighbour reporting seeing me in a car full of Asian men. She also remembered the abusive and racist calls to our landline. She could not forget the many times I'd come home bruised and battered. She knew I was sexually active, and she knew I was taking drugs. Slowly, she was piecing it all together. And yet still, the police insisted there was nothing they could do.

"Look, if your daughter is going out of her own free will, we can't exactly drag her back home," they pointed out.

"Maybe you could try keeping her indoors?" another suggested. "That's what I'd do, if it was my daughter. Don't let her out. Simple."

I was labelled as a troublesome teenager, gone off the rails, in with the wrong crowd... I heard it over and over again. I might as well have had 'Trouble' branded across my face. Nobody once suggested that I might be a victim. It didn't occur to anyone that I might be being groomed, exploited, sexually, physically and mentally abused.

Even the police thought I was a time waster. And despite me skipping school and getting myself into all sorts of scrapes, there was no meaningful involvement with social services. Maybe they thought I was a waste of time too. I was a child, totally on my own. So what chance did I have?

* * * *

If we were not being carted, like cattle, to different locations to be abused, then sometimes our abusers came to us. At one party, I was raped by a man who had been brought from Leicester, apparently especially to see me. I felt like some sort of sleazy tourist attraction, and I knew I was supposed to feel grateful, special even, when he said:

"I've come a long way, just to see you…"

He was almost drooling over me as he spoke, and I tried not to gag. I didn't feel special. I had never felt so pitiful and valueless in my entire life. Yet the misery and chaos of the parties continued.

One night, I was raped by a man who was easily in his late 40s, and old enough to be my father. Afterwards, I walked home in a daze and didn't sleep a wink all night. The following morning, a Sunday, Dad popped his head round my bedroom door.

"Get dressed! I'm taking you out for a Wetherspoon breakfast," he said. "Little treat."

Normally, I loved going out for breakfast with Dad. But, as Dad tucked into his food, I found it hard even to sip my orange juice. All I could think of was the abuse the night before; of the man who had raped me, who was a similar age to my own dad. How could I switch from being raped to eating breakfast, a few hours later, as though I hadn't a care in the world? And yet somehow, I did it. Dad's happiness and enthusiasm was infectious. So, with a huge effort, I shoved the abuse into the far recesses of my mind, and I painted on a smile.

"Eat up," Dad smiled, nicking a sausage off my plate. "Do you want another slice of toast?"

Again, I was precariously balancing the two sides of my

life, walking an emotional and practical tightrope. I knew I couldn't do this forever. But I also could not see an end to it.

On another night, I was taken to a house where a man showed me upstairs and ushered me into a bedroom.

"My mother is asleep in the room next door," the man whispered. "So don't even think about making any noise. Be quiet."

He made me get into a bed with him and he raped me silently. But before he was finished, the bedroom door opened a little and an elderly lady poked her head around. Quietly, I slid down the bed, under the covers, lying as flat and as still as I could. I barely dared breathe as she exchanged a few words with her son, before leaving again.

"Well done, Tina," he whispered. "I'll get you some doner meat later."

I might just as well have been a dog, getting a pat on the head and a treat for good behaviour. A reward for keeping my mouth shut. Afterwards, I was packed off home with a bag of meat. Another night's work done.

'Good girl,' Pretos texted me later.

The message gave me a sense of relief. But, as always, it was temporary.

'Party tomoz,' he continued. 'B ready.'

The following night, at yet another party at yet another house, the vodka flowed and the drugs were passed around like sweets. Dreamily, I thought back to how parties used to be, in my former life. I remembered a big family party, when I was small, and a big pink cake. Another year, there was a princess birthday cake, and a princess dressing up outfit, just for me. I'd been to swimming parties, magician parties and kids' discos in the Irish centre. One year, I'd had a Mr Blobby party and my parents had hired out the function room of the local pub. I was thrilled when Mr Blobby turned up in his pink and yellow spotty costume, and I raced around the pub, looking for my favourite uncle, Pete, so that he could meet Mr Blobby in person.

"Uncle Pete!" I yelled. "Where are you? Come and see Mr Blobby!"

But Uncle Pete was nowhere to be found. It wasn't until Mr Blobby waved his goodbyes that my uncle miraculously appeared, looking rather hot and sweaty!

"You missed Mr Blobby!" I said reproachfully.

I didn't make the connection for many years afterwards and it became a joke in the family. They were all such happy memories, such great parties. But the word was sullied now ruined beyond repair.

"Come on Tina, get this down you," Manny laughed, handing me a bottle of vodka. "You look miles away. Join the party!"

I sighed. If I never attended another party in my entire life, it would be too soon. But of course, just a few days later, Pretos organised yet another party; yet another rape.

10

Pregnant

At the start of April 2007, I noticed I was feeling sluggish and exhausted in the mornings. It was not surprising, given the stress I was under, and so I thought nothing of it. The abusive calls and visits to our home had gradually eased off because I was doing exactly as I was told by the gang. But I knew that the situation could quite easily be reversed, and the knowledge was always there, my stomach was always clenched, my heart beating just that little bit faster. Even at 15, I knew it wasn't good for my health. Besides, I was smoking, drinking alcohol and taking drugs several times a week. I was hardly looking after myself.

"You don't look too well," Mum remarked one evening, placing her hand on my forehead. "No fever though. Let's keep an eye on you."

I was sleeping more than usual yet exhausted every morning when the alarm went off. I found I couldn't wait to get home from my work for the gang, just so that I could collapse under my duvet and sleep some more.

"You sure you're okay?" Mum asked, giving me a hard stare.

I nodded listlessly, too tired to say anything more. But a couple of weeks on, she came into my bedroom and opened my top drawer. She pulled out a sealed packet of sanitary pads and, in that moment, everything fell into place. I knew exactly why I was feeling exhausted and nauseous. I knew precisely why I hadn't opened last month's sanitary towels.

"I think you may be pregnant," Mum said, each word loaded with dismay.

I couldn't look at her. I was so scared. I felt like such a failure, such a disappointment, as a daughter.

"Who's the father?" she asked me, and her voice was gentler now. "Please, Christina, I need to know. You are still a child."

Again, I hung my head, and the tears stung my eyes. The awful, scandalous, truth was, I had absolutely no idea. The realisation that the father could be one of maybe a dozen men was so shocking, so shaming, that I felt myself physically folding and shutting out the world. I felt utterly worthless. Back then, I believed the shame and the scandal was all mine.

"We need to make an appointment with the GP," Mum said.

It felt surreal, sitting there, a few days later, with my chemistry folder in my lap, requesting a termination.

"I can't see any other option," I told the doctor.

I was relieved that Mum had accepted the decision without argument; we were Roman Catholic and so it was not an easy choice for either of us. But I could not have brought a child of rape into the world when I was still just a child myself.

In the days that followed, as I waited for my hospital appointment to come through, I confided in one of the girls.

"Don't tell anyone," I pleaded.

But it wasn't a secret for long. Pretos pulled me to one side and confronted me.

"Is this right?" he asked. "You're pregnant?"

I shrugged, unsure whether to tell the truth or not. But if I thought being pregnant might exempt me from the abuse, then I was wrong. There was no consideration, no sympathy, no special treatment. I was made to carry on exactly as normal.

"You'd better get rid of it," Pretos told me.

"I am," I replied. "Next week."

That night, he texted, threatening to kill me if I backed out of the abortion.

"I promise I won't," I replied.

But that wasn't enough for him. The vile messages continued, and he threatened to hurt my parents too. I was a bundle of nerves, fearful each time they went to work, in case they didn't come back. On the morning of my appointment, I got another chilling text.

'I will be watchin. get it done. or else.'

I had asked Macie, and not Mum, to come to Halifax Hospital with me. I couldn't bear to see Mum's face as I was wheeled away for the procedure. I didn't think I'd go through with it if she was with me.

In the morning, Macie and I downed as much vodka as we could stomach, and I smoked a joint. It was grossly inappropriate behaviour, preceding something so sombre and life changing as an abortion. I would live to regret that. I would live to regret it all.

In my defence, if there is any, I was 15 years old and I wanted to take the edge off my angst. I was mixed-up, drugged up and terrified. Pretos' threats swarmed around my head like wasps over and over. I had to have the termination. I had no choice, in this, or in anything else. I wasn't able to look after myself, never mind a baby. I felt coerced into the abortion, by the gang and also by myself.

"Christina O'Connor," I mumbled as I arrived at reception.

The paperwork had already been signed and processed. All that remained was for me to subject my body to yet more trauma. Somehow, I got through it, pretending it wasn't happening, telling myself this wasn't me at all.

When I got home, Mum tucked me into bed and made me a hot chocolate. I was doubled over with what felt like stomach cramps and, at first, I focused only on the physical pain. And then on the relief, which crashed over me like a wave. It was over. I was no longer pregnant. I texted Pretos and he texted back with his approval:

'Good girl.'

But as the days passed, the dull ache in my abdomen grew and ballooned into a gaping chasm, a horrible emptiness. The realisation of what I had done hit me a little more, each day, hacking away at my soul. I was eaten up with guilt and regret.

I worked out that my baby would have been due in late November, just before Christmas. For some reason, though I would never know for sure, I was convinced my unborn baby was a little girl; a daughter. I ran through possible names in my head.

'Grace, Olivia, Mia…'

I like Grace, I decided. Gracie. I would call her Gracie. But christening her and talking to her only served to make her seem more real, more present. She took shape in my mind. And my grief became increasingly raw. I found myself biting back tears in the supermarket as I walked past rows of little pink dresses and girly outfits. Would she have been an Irish dancer? Or a tomboy? A chocoholic? A Disney fan? I would never know. Would she tap her fingers, as I did, when I was nervous? Would she enjoy baking soda bread, like me? I imagined a miniature version of myself. I tortured myself with details and dreams, and slowly, it pulled me apart.

"I'm sorry, Gracie," I sobbed.

My baby was not here, I had never met her, yet still, I felt as though I was her mother. I would always be her mother. It was heartbreaking, thinking of what might have been, dwelling on how differently my life – and hers, especially hers – might have turned out.

Mum and I had agreed not to tell Dad about my pregnancy; we had thought it would upset him unnecessarily. I couldn't bear to see the hurt in his eyes, not on top of everything else. And so we never mentioned the baby in our house, and it was as though she had never even existed. I was offered counselling by the GP but I refused it. I didn't feel like any outsider could even begin to understand what I was going through. And I didn't see the point of talking. Talking would not bring my baby Gracie back. Talking would not make Pretos disappear.

Predictably, the gang showed me no sympathy and I was expected to be back out, as normal, within a few days.

'Pick u up 7 ish' Pretos texted. 'Busy nite 4 u.'

After the termination, my GP had insisted I consider some form of birth control, and I opted to try the contraceptive injection, instead of the pill. But again, I began to gain weight steadily and I grew mistrustful. I was supposed to attend three monthly appointments, but I missed many of those, because I was either drunk or drugged or out of town with the gang. My lifestyle was so chaotic that keeping to any kind of schedule was a challenge I usually could not meet. Despite having been through the anguish of the termination, I did not dwell on the possibility of falling pregnant again. I just didn't believe that lightning would strike me twice.

The weeks passed, and I parcelled up my grief and locked it away. But the memory of baby Gracie was always there, itching to get out. Over time, the rawness eased a little. But the pain and the longing remained. And the guilt? Well, that just seemed to get worse and worse.

Each time I saw a pram, I'd torment myself with images of how my own baby daughter might have looked by now; would she be smiling and rolling over? Sleeping through the night? I didn't want to forget my baby; it felt wrong to pretend she had never existed. Yet remembering her was unbearable. But I deserved this, I reminded myself. This was all my fault. I drank more and more, getting myself paralytically drunk each night to blot out the recriminations in my mind. And so, though the gang had caused my suffering, I relied on them, and their steady stream of vodka and Jack Daniels, to ease my agony.

* * * *

That summer, I started seeing a new 'boyfriend', one of the gang, named Beastie. He was in his 20s so quite a few years older than me. I was not yet 16. In return for a medicinal supply of booze and drugs, I did exactly as he told me. And I was under no illusions, after my 'relationship' with Glen, that having a boyfriend would give me some sort of exemption from the sexual demands of the gang. If anything, Beastie seemed to like loaning me out, passing me around his friends, like I was a cannabis joint or a packet of mints. I was there to be used and abused at will.

And still, running alongside, my normal life continued. I left school, without even sitting most of my GCSE exams. I knew I had no hope of passing and so self-sabotage seemed like the most attractive option. My education, like my childhood, had been flushed away into the sewers and there was no way it could be fished back out. At the end of June 2007, I went to the school leaving prom, along with the rest of my class. Mum bought me a pink dress, with darker coloured netting over the bodice, and a hem that came to just below my knee.

"Oh, you look beautiful," Mum and Dad beamed, snapping photos as I posed shyly in the hallway.

I felt like such a fake. Despite everything, they were immensely and unconditionally proud of me. And, pushing my cares aside, for that one evening, I had a brilliant time at the prom, dancing and laughing with my old friends from school. All animosities between us were wiped away, for one night only. It was a rare chance to be a normal teenager.

Late that week, I passed my prom photos around the gang members, as though it was a perfectly normal thing to do. As though they were nothing more than kindly uncles or benevolent acquaintances.

"Nice," they said. "You look good, Tina."

One by one, they admired my dress and my hair, just as anyone else would. These occasions, when my two lives bled into one another, just served to make my confusion worse. I questioned who I was, and which version of me was the real one – if any? I doubted my sense of self. The disparity between who I was at home and who I was with the gang was so great that I could not reconcile the two.

I gathered my photos back into the folder and then it was on with the business of the day; me obeying orders, me carrying out sex acts. What I could not have known was that the gap, in the future, would be stretched out wider still. And one day, I would break into two.

****

After I turned 16, that August, the interminable rows with my parents intensified. I had failed all of my GCSE exams, which, though no surprise, had caused more trouble for me at home.

"What about your future?" Mum asked. "What are you

going to do with your life? You're throwing your prospects away."

I wasn't even listening. I couldn't see it then, but I had thrown nothing away. My prospects had been stolen from me, ripped from my hands. Again and again, I begged to be allowed to move to Ireland, but my parents wouldn't hear of it.

"Things would be different in Kerry," I pleaded. "I promise. Just let me go, please."

"How?" Mum demanded. "How would they be different? And if you can improve your behaviour in Ireland, why can't you improve it here? It makes no sense.

"You'll have to prove yourself first. Show us that you can turn this around, Christina. No more drinking, no more late nights. No more secret boyfriends."

I glared at her and marched out of the room.

"I hate living here!" I yelled, grabbing my coat, and slamming the front door shut.

I felt as though Mum was pushing me back into the claws of the gang. I was left with nowhere else to turn. I couldn't take my anger out on the gang and so, unfairly and irrationally, I downloaded it all onto my parents instead. Looking back now, I can see she and Dad were in an impossible situation, and they must have been out of their minds with concern for me. But all I could think about was who I'd have to have sex with later that day, in order to keep me and my family safe.

11

Drug Debt

One night, aged 16, I was taken to the house of a man nicknamed Chiller. He persuaded me to go outside and get into his Mercedes with him, where he forced me to have sex. As I was getting out afterwards, he handed me a bag of cannabis worth £10. I was grateful, because smoking made me relax, and helped me to sleep at night. Smoking was a way of blocking out the horror. I could smoke a joint out of my bedroom window and then blame the smell of weed on our neighbours, a few doors down, who were notorious for smoking what my parents called 'wacky baccy'. Whenever Mum complained about the whiff of cannabis, I would agree and point the finger further down the street.

"Blame them," I'd tell her, though I am not sure she ever believed me.

I thought I had 'earned' the drugs from Chiller, as always. But the following day, he texted to tell me I owed him £10, which of course I didn't have. I hadn't had pocket money at home for so long, because of my poor behaviour. I relied completely on Pretos for drugs, booze and cigarettes.

'Pay up, or it's £20,' he wrote.

I didn't worry too much at first. The gang members were always making violent threats and outlandish demands. Mostly, those threats melted away after they got what they wanted. I felt sure Chiller would soon get bored with me and move onto bullying someone else. But a few days later, I got a message demanding £30. Then it shot up to £40.

"I don't have the money," I told him. "Please leave me alone."

I was used to being forced into performing sex acts for so-called drug or food debts. It had become a way of life for me. But this was different. Chiller knew I didn't have the money. Instead, he was thoroughly enjoying watching me squirm, picking on me and singling me out of the group, and I struggled and shrivelled under the pressure. It was like being 11 years old in the high school playground, all over again.

Hey fatty!

The rest of the gang joined in too. Every day, I was reminded that my debt was rising. And rising. This was just a bit of sport for them. But it was crushing me.

"I can't pay it," I said desperately. "You know I can't."

One night, Pretos messaged and told me to meet him outside my house. When I got into the car, I was pinned against the back seat. There were two other girls in the car too.

"You're not getting away with this," he snarled.

Pretos screeched off, at speed, refusing to let me out of the car.

"Please!" I begged. "I'm scared now. Just let me go."

He raced around the streets before coming to a sudden stop, and the other girls got out of the car. When I tried to follow, I felt punches raining down on my head. I fell to the ground at the side of the road, screaming and begging to be left alone. In the mayhem, I grabbed hold of a mobile phone and dialled 999.

"Help!" I yelled. "Help!"

The blood poured from my nose and blurred my vision as I was bundled back in the car, this time without the other girls, and Pretos drove away once again. As I curled into a ball on the back seat, with my whole body throbbing in agony, he continued to scream at me.

"You're a piece of shit. White shit."

Eventually, I was dumped on the pavement, like a scrap of litter, and he drove off. Shaking, I was able to find my own phone, zipped safely into a pocket, and I called my dad. When he arrived in the truck, he was outraged.

"Who did this?" he asked. "Pet, please tell us what's going on."

He took me home and Mum bathed my cuts and bruises, her tears rolling down her cheeks and splashing onto the bathroom floor. It turned out that the phone I had earlier used to call the police belonged to one of the girls. They had traced it and turned up at the girl's home, but her family knew nothing of any attack and so the call was considered a hoax. Luckily, Dad had come to my rescue. Yet again. I had escaped the gang this once. But I knew that wasn't the end of it.

Terrified of seeing Pretos again, I tried hiding out at home, switching off my phone, hoping against hope that they would somehow forget I had ever existed. But the dread was always there, setting and solidifying inside my stomach like a hard cement. The fear perched on my shoulder like a black crow.

'Get out now,' Pretos texted. 'Or else.'

I'd had enough beatings off Pretos to know that he wasn't bluffing. A couple of days later, still with a line of bruises across my back, I agreed to meet up with the gang.

"Don't think you're getting away with this, slag," one of the men said, as I got into the car.

Later that afternoon, we were driving through Huddersfield, when my phone rang.

"Your dad's had a bit of an accident," Mum told me. "The wheel's come off his truck. Literally just rolled down the slip road as he was driving onto the M62."

I clapped my hand to my mouth in alarm.

"Is he okay?" I gasped.

"Yes, he's fine, don't worry," she reassured me. "No casualties. He could have been killed, or he could have killed someone else. He was so lucky.

"Anyway, he's waiting for a recovery truck, and then I'm going to pick him up. So we won't be at home when you get back. I'm just making sure you have your key."

I put the phone down, thankful that there were no injuries. Then one of the men smirked and said to me:

"Did the wheel come off your dad's truck then?"

I nodded, astonished.

"How do you…?" I began.

My stomach plummeted and my back prickled as though

an army of ants was marching down my spine. Suddenly, it all made perfect sense. I knew full well this was no accident. This was the gang's way of keeping me in line and telling me to obey orders. He jabbed his finger at me and said nastily:

"Maybe now, you'll listen, and you'll do as you're told."

Mutely, I nodded. I knew how evil these men were. I knew they were debased, violent, inhumane. Even so, I was shocked that they would target my family so blatantly and with such high stakes. I should have been furious, convulsed with rage, on behalf of my dad. Instead, oddly, I became even more compliant and obedient. I was so frightened that I saw it as the only option.

"Sorry," I muttered. "Really sorry."

When I got home that night, Dad was in the kitchen.

"Are you okay?" I asked, throwing myself into his arms.

"Don't look so worried, pet," he smiled. "We're all safe. No harm done. That's the main issue. It was just one of those things."

But this was not just one of those things. I knew also that this was the start, and not the end. Days later, our living room window was smashed. That same night, a brick came through the front door.

"What the hell?" Dad complained, as he swept up the broken glass. "Who is doing this?"

He and Mum called the police, realising now that the loose wheel was probably not a freak accident after all.

"Would anyone want to target you?" asked the officers. "And any idea who? Or why?"

They shook their heads, mystified. They didn't have any

enemies. They just weren't the sort. Part of me was terrified of the police linking this to me, but a bigger part of me longed for them to do so. I wanted – needed – a way out. I was drowning, with my head below the water. I needed a life raft.

Dad worked late into the night, boarding up the windows, making the house secure again. But even so, I lay awake right through to the dawn, jumping at every small crack and creak. I was afraid for my life, and for my parents' lives. At 16 it was a weighty load to carry alone.

Early the next morning, I went out, petrified at what might happen next. And I was right to worry. In the weeks that followed, our windows were smashed again. Dad replaced them all himself, but next the house was pelted with rotten eggs and sludge.

"Probably just kids," Dad reassured me as he hosed away the mess. "They'll move onto a new house soon enough. Don't dwell on it."

"Yeah," I mumbled. "I hope you're right."

One morning, Mum was on a late start at work, but when I saw her later, she was pale and shaken.

"I had a problem with my car on the way in," she explained. "The wheel came loose, as I was driving. Sounds like the same thing that happened to your dad. I can't believe it! Who would do something like that?

"We must have a complete maniac in the neighbourhood."

Anger bubbled up inside me. How dare they target my parents like this? But it was quickly stifled by an ice-cold fear. What next? Would they only stop when one of us was dead? The campaign was escalating, way out of control, way beyond anything I'd known before.

The terror completely took over my life. I couldn't concentrate. I couldn't even hold a conversation. My friends were chatting about a new mascara. I was panicking about my family being killed. There was no middle ground. In despair, I called Pretos.

"Please leave my parents alone," I pleaded. "I'll do whatever you want. Just leave them alone."

"Or else what?" he replied. "If you don't behave, your mum gets it. Ha ha. We rape your mum instead, what about that?"

He laughed loudly, for the benefit of his back seat audience, or possibly just for himself.

"I can meet you later on," I offered. "Anything. I'll do anything. I don't mind."

That night, and every night which followed, I had no choice but to go out and have sex with strangers, to protect my family. Christina had gone and a machine, a mere commodity, had taken her place. I was a child with the weight and the worries of the world on my shoulders. I hated the gang, but they were all I had.

* * * *

Meanwhile, though there were no outright acts of violence, the campaign against my family home simmered and bubbled, like a witch's broth. For weeks, the gang left us alone, but I suspected they were just lulling me into a false sense of security. Even so, I would allow myself, despite the warning bells, to believe that they had forgotten about my debt to Chiller and had moved onto someone else. I wanted so much for it to be true.

So when they smashed another window or called the house phone with a volley of sick abuse, it had so much more impact and I was left reeling every time. My parents were becoming more and more bewildered and afraid. And though they knew that I was lying to them, they didn't know the truth either. They had no idea who was behind the attacks, or why.

Mum picked up calls in which members of the gang threatened to rape her or kill her. We came home sometimes to find the neighbours telling us there had been a disturbance outside our home, with people shouting and banging on the door.

"Sorry," Dad told them. "We've been having some problems lately. Not sure what's behind it all. Really sorry."

It broke my heart that, on top of everything else he had to endure, he felt the need to apologise too.

One evening, we arrived home, and Mum spotted something on the doorstep.

"Looks like a parcel," she said, as she locked the car. "I'm not expecting a delivery."

But as we got nearer, she suddenly frowned and stopped dead. There, leaning against our front door, was a funeral wreath.

"This must have been delivered to the wrong address," she said. "How awful."

She picked it up to search for a name or a label, but I just stood and stared, my mouth hanging slack with shock. I knew exactly who the wreath was for. But as usual, I couldn't tell her.

"Can you knock and ask the neighbours, love?" Mum said. "Make sure nobody has ordered a wreath? We need to find out who this belongs to."

I went through the motions of checking with our neighbours on either side, knowing it was completely futile, but following Mum's wishes with my nerves jangling and my heart pounding. I felt like I was walking towards the edge of a sheer drop.

"Well, it's a mystery," Mum proclaimed, later that evening. "I just don't know who this belongs to."

But I didn't need any further explanation or warning. I knew exactly what was required of me and I knew what would happen if I didn't comply.

Each time there was an attack on our house, my parents called the police, and through witness accounts, they had eventually identified a suspect.

"We believe an Asian male is responsible for organising some of these attacks," an officer explained. "We're planning an arrest."

Later, he showed us a photo, and my insides twisted with alarm. It was one of the gang.

My parents were baffled; they obviously didn't know him, though they had seen him hanging around our street. There was, as yet no link to me, and no suggestion of a motive, but I was terrified of the police digging further and implicating me. Ironically, a wider investigation would have been exactly the thing to save me, yet I feared it would be the end of me. Perhaps it could have been both.

The gang member was charged with witness intimidation and later convicted. My parents were pleased; they saw this as justice and hoped it signalled the end of the trouble. The rest of the gang now had another reason to target me. As well as owing them money, I was considered a police grass.

And so it went on. And on.

On New Year's Eve 2007, Mum and Dad went to the Irish Centre to celebrate, as they did every year. Most 16-year-olds were probably out at 'parties', in the traditional sense, sneaking their first taste of Baileys Irish Cream, sharing a first kiss with a boy they'd fancied right through school. But I was beyond all that. The word 'party' sent a seismic tremor through me. Besides, I was used to sinking a half-bottle of vodka to myself, and with it a couple of ecstasy pills. I'd had more sexual partners than the whole of my year group put together. Once, I'd thought all that was cool. But now, at New Year, whilst my peers all celebrated, it held no appeal for me.

I was the girl with everything, and the girl with nothing at all.

Instead, whilst my parents were out, I'd arranged for a couple of the girls to come round for a quiet night. They'd nipped off to the shop at the petrol station to buy chocolate and lemonade and so I was in the house on my own. I hadn't seen the gang for a few days because I'd been with my family for Christmas and, with my parents off work, it was hard to get away. I was under pressure to go out and meet Pretos, but it was tricky because I seemed to be busy every day, visiting relatives and family friends.

'Will b out after Xmas' I had texted. 'Promise.'

With my pals out, that New Year's Eve, I nipped upstairs to the loo. But as I closed the bathroom door, there were two loud bangs, splitting the night air, followed by the tinkling and shattering of glass.

I dashed downstairs, convinced one of my friends had come back and somehow fallen through a pane of glass in the door. But as I reached the hallway, the house was eerily silent. And cold too. There was an unsettling breeze around my legs and I shivered and hugged my arms around my chest.

"Hello?" I said, in a small voice.

Creeping forwards, towards the front window, I felt my slippers crunching on broken glass. I lifted the edge of the curtain and gasped. There was nothing there. The whole pane of glass had gone. Swivelling around in panic, I remembered the loud bangs, a little like fireworks, *a lot like gunshots*, and my stomach flipped.

I turned back, towards the kitchen, which was in direct line with the window. In the cupboard doors, there were two small holes, with fine cracks radiating outwards. As I fumbled with my phone, I felt myself retching with fright.

"Mum!" I gasped. "Someone is shooting at the house! Please come home!"

"What?" she asked, struggling to hear me.

There was music and laughter in the background, sounds of enjoyment and celebration, and it jarred horribly with the silent living room, covered in broken glass and me cowering on the floor, in case I was shot at again.

"Come home!" I yelled. "Please!"

She and Dad rushed back, thankfully in just a few minutes. When my two friends got back from the shop, with armfuls of goodies, they were packed off home; our get-together abandoned. The police arrived soon afterwards.

"Can you tell me what happened?" asked an officer.

"Not really," I shuddered. "I was upstairs in the bathroom. I heard gunshots. I came down to find the window smashed and bullet holes in the cupboards."

Much as I wanted this to end, I was terrified also of the police identifying the culprits and uncovering the rest of my secret life.

"It's New Year's Eve," he said. "People do crazy stuff on the last day of the year. It may be gunshots, it may just be an air rifle."

It was at once a relief and also a huge frustration that he didn't seem to be taking it as seriously as I'd expected.

"We have bullet holes in our kitchen cupboards," Mum reminded him.

The officer promised to do all he could. But he was already receiving details of his next call out on his radio.

"Busy night," he apologised. "I have to go."

None of us slept at all that night; Mum and Dad kept a vigil in the living room, and I lay on my bed, stiff and cold, my skin crawling with anxiety. Vicky mewed, agitatedly, at the side of my bed. Even our cat was scared. I was in such a mess.

Our family plans for New Year's Day were cancelled; we just didn't feel it was safe to leave the house unattended.

"Christina, I want you to be honest, and tell me what's going on," Mum said. "For the hundredth time, I know you know more about all this than you're admitting."

It was another chance to unburden myself and to confide in her. But the terror of what might happen if I did, was greater than my fear of her reaction. And so, I said nothing.

But if Mum was becoming suspicious, it seemed the police were not. I had been interviewed several times, for apparent muggings, street assaults, attacks on my home and on my parents' cars. On many occasions, I had been picked up late at night, wandering the streets, and brought home by the police. Yet they never questioned why I, a regular teenager, seemed to be at the epicentre of some sort of crime epidemic. I was the common denominator here. Yet they just never noticed.

* * * *

In the early part of 2008, the rows with my parents became unbearable. Mum interrogated me over and over about the gang and she just wouldn't let it go. She was, of course, be-having like any responsible parent. But I didn't want to hear it.

"Christina, there's something going wrong here every week," she said. "I know you're telling me lies. I want to know the truth. Please."

Again, I was tempted to speak out. Again, I was too afraid.

Instead, I moved out of the house. I could take no more. I was worried about my parents' safety too; I felt as though I was bringing danger to their door. At least this way, I could deflect the attention away from their address and onto mine. I found a little bedsit not far from our family home and I got a job working on a butcher's stall in the local market hall. I enjoyed it at first and tried to keep my work secret from the gang. I just wanted a little piece of my life for myself, away from their toxic coercion. But it didn't take long for someone to spot me behind the counter, and Pretos and his pals turned up one afternoon as I was serving customers.

"She's nice, Tina, isn't she?" one of them said loudly. "Sexy, you know. Bit of a tease."

There were a few uncomfortable murmurs in the queue and my boss glared at me.

"Tell your friends to go away," he said. "They're putting my customers off."

I was mortified and managed to persuade them to leave. But a few days later, they reappeared, this time urging my boss to check the money in the till.

"She's a bit light fingered," they explained. "You might have trouble with her. She's a little thief."

They were laughing as they said it, but I could tell my boss didn't get the joke at all. I lost my job that same week and I was back in the clutches of the gang, all day, every day. That little branch of independence, that small step towards normality, was stamped out.

One night, I was taken to yet another party, and afterwards, for a reason I couldn't fathom, one of the men got violent with me, slapping me about and kicking me. I managed to get out of the house, but he followed me and snatched my phone. He threw it high in the air, and it landed on the roof of a nearby chicken factory, way out of my reach.

"Good luck getting that back," he sneered, before sauntering off in the other direction.

I stumbled down the street, tears of despair rolling down my cheeks, diluting the blood leaking from my busted nose. It wasn't really much different to so many other parties, to so many other nights. But as the cold air hit me, I was overcome with a wave of hopelessness and misery. I felt as though I couldn't carry on. I spotted a phone box at the end of the road and called the police.

"I've been assaulted," I sobbed. "I need help. Someone help me please."

Sinking to my knees in the phone box, I waited. The police car turned up soon afterwards, and the officers were kind enough to have a look on the factory roof for my phone, but they couldn't find it. Afterwards, they took me to hospital.

"Get yourself checked out," they said. "Some of those bruises look nasty."

I called Dad from a payphone outside A&E, and he came to collect me. Afterwards he insisted on me staying the night at our family home. On the journey back, he told me he had seen a commotion outside the chicken factory, with the police parked at the roadside, but he hadn't realised his own daughter was at the centre of it.

"I wish I'd known," he said. "I could have spoken to the police and lodged a formal complaint."

But the incident went no further. The police didn't take a statement or investigate as far as I knew. By now, I was just one of a number of troublesome kids, gone off the rails, in with the wrong crowd, beyond salvation. I knew the spiel off by heart.

There was one police officer who, whenever he came across me and the other girls late at night, would always give me a lift home and make sure I was safe. He even took us all to McDonald's, to cheer us up.

"You girls shouldn't be wandering the streets," he told us. "It's too dangerous. Come on, I'll buy you all a burger and a hot tea."

He showed us such care and kindness. He never judged or lectured us. I don't even remember his name now, but I will never forget his face and I will always be grateful. There was so little compassion in my world, and he was a shining light, a glimmer of hope in my darkness.

12

Locked Up

Even though I was officially living in the bedsit, I often found myself back at home. Mum brought food round, and Dad was always offering me money and giving me lifts. He still drove around at night, looking for me, just as he always had. Around six months on, after well-intentioned pleas from my parents, I decided to move back home permanently.

"We worry about you," Dad told me. "We need to know that you're safe. We want you here."

Ironically, I was no safer at home than I was in the bedsit. I was the problem – not the solution. But he didn't know that.

I got a new job, in a sandwich shop, but the gang turned up to torment me again, and I lost that role too. I found work babysitting, then I got a job at the Irish Centre, helping out with catering and cleaning. I was never out of work for long, but I was never in work for long either. The gang saw to that. Each time I settled in at a new place, they turned up to make a scene.

And, as much as I told myself that I wanted to break away, I was reliant on them too. When my phone broke, Pretos was always ready with a new one. He bought me takeaways, alcohol, cigarettes and drugs. My days were planned out by the gang. My life was totally under their control. I didn't even have to think for myself. At times, I loathed it, at times, I craved it. And it was all I knew.

Having been overweight as a child, I was now much slimmer and wore lots of make-up. I had turned 17 and, like most teenagers, I trowelled on layers of orange foundation, along with too much eyeshadow and eyeliner. I loved the attention it brought me. I couldn't avoid having sex with the gang members, and so I consoled myself by thinking I was beautiful and that was why they wanted me. I couldn't avoid them ruling my life, and so I told myself they loved me and that was why they gave me drugs and cigarettes. I kept on telling myself these things but that didn't mean that, deep down, I believed them. It was very hard to lie to myself. Yet I had to convince myself I was better off with them because I could not get rid of them. And I thought, too, that nobody else would ever want me. I heard of girls I'd gone to school with hooking up with boys their own age. They were enjoying the various stages of traditional dating; meals out, saving for holidays, mortgages even. A few had got engaged. But I knew all of that was out of bounds for me. I was damaged goods, tarnished, chipped, cracked and beyond repair. I was stuck with the gang, and they were stuck with me.

One day, as we drove through Huddersfield, Pretos pulled in at the side of the road.

"Go and rob a bag," he said. "And don't mess me about."

I had no idea who he was talking to.

"You two," he said, nodding at me and another of the girls. "Go on. A bag. Or a phone."

I stared at him. At first, I thought he was joking. I had never stolen anything in my life before. My worst transgression so far was taking the money from Dad's safe in the basement and I always promised myself I would replace that, as soon as I could afford it. I certainly didn't go around mugging people. But then we were given a small steak knife each and it suddenly became horribly real. This was no joke. The blade of the knife was cold and smooth in my palm. He handed them out as though they were everyday accessories. As though every teenage girl carried her own personal steak knife.

"Go on!" he snapped.

There was a familiar gleam in his eye which reminded me I didn't dare disobey. We climbed out of the car, giggling with bravado, neither of us with any idea of what to do. I had no clue of the actual mechanics of theft. We spotted a woman walking towards us, with bags over her arm, and, against all of my instincts, I ran at her with the knife in my hand. Screwing my eyes tight, and whispering a silent apology, I yanked a bag from her arm and continued running at pace.

"Well done girls," Pretos laughed, rifling through the bag in the car. "Who fancies kebab and chips?"

I felt so nauseous that I couldn't eat a thing. I replayed snatching the bag, over and over in my mind. I heard her gulp in astonishment before she screamed at the top of her voice. I had used a knife to steal from a complete stranger. I had threatened her. I was an armed robber. The realisation knocked me sick.

'Well done girls!'

The very next afternoon, the police came to my family home. They told me that my name had been put forward and that I matched the description of one of two females who had carried out a violent street robbery. It did not occur to me then that perhaps – just perhaps – the very people who had encouraged me to commit the crime were the same ones who had anonymously passed my name to the police. I was questioned and released conditionally, knowing that charges would surely follow.

On a summer's evening in 2009, a few weeks before I turned 18, I was out with the gang as usual. One of the men pointed out a woman walking alone in the opposite direction.

"Her," he said. "Go and take her bag."

I shifted uncomfortably. I hated this. Yet I knew I couldn't say no. The fear of retaliation, physical, mental and sexual, overpowered and smothered everything else. Yet as I looked at the woman, I saw she was older than my mum and she had that same careworn, kindly face too. I knew I couldn't do it.

"I've got a better idea," I blurted out suddenly. "I've got the keys to an empty house. I can take you there and we'll rob it."

Mum and her best pal had keys to each other's homes, in case of an emergency, or whilst the other was on holiday. The keys had hung on a hook in our hallway for years, alongside our own keys. Mum's friend worked night shifts and so I knew that her house was empty overnight.

"Honestly, it's easy money," I said convincingly. "She has a games console. Loads of stuff."

Even as the words left my mouth, I knew it was outrageous. And cruel. And also laughably stupid. But it was too late now. I was already spilling out the address and suggesting suitable dates.

"We'll do it tonight," one of the men said.

My heart was thumping. I couldn't believe what I had got myself into. Caught between pleasing the gang and clinging onto my own decency, I had failed the test spectacularly. It was agreed that I would burgle the house, along with another girl and one of the gang members. I told myself, as I got ready at home, that I didn't care about the burglary. That this was just one more disaster in my car-crash life. I shut out the voices which told me that there was simply no way back from this. That it was depraved and disgusting. That I was losing my humanity, just like the gang. I was becoming one of them.

That evening, I slipped out of the house and met up with the others. As we got to the street where Mum's mate lived, I fumbled in my pocket for the keys.

"Don't be daft," hissed the gang member. "We need to make it look real."

I watched in dismay as he kicked the back door in. I hadn't bargained for this. I hadn't anticipated any damage or mess. With a heavy heart, I climbed through the door frame, picking my way through the broken shards of glass and wood. Then the other girl and I scurried around the house, like rodents, stealing a games console and a bundle of cash.

"Let's get out." I urged her. "Quick as you can."

As we left, minutes later, I felt absolutely desolate. We handed the money and console over to the gang, and I ran back home. I had a sick feeling inside. I knew I would never get away with this. And a part of me didn't want to get away with it either. I deserved punishment. The next day, predictably, the police came.

"You were seen by a neighbour," Mum told me tearfully. "And I know you took the keys. Honestly Christina, I don't know what to say. She's my friend, you've known her since you were a baby.

"What the hell is wrong with you?"

Dad said very little, but I knew he was hurting. I had brought shame and humiliation onto my whole family.

* * * *

Mum and I were at home one night, and Dad was out, when Pretos texted to tell me to meet him.

"I need to go out," I told her. "I won't be long."

Her face fell.

"Please don't," she replied. "I thought we could have a nice night in, watch a film?"

I sighed. I texted Pretos, telling him I couldn't make it. But I didn't think for a minute he would accept that.

"Let's make a hot chocolate," Mum suggested. "Any ideas for a film?"

My phone bleeped insistently in my pocket and an unease crept over me. Soon my palms were sweating, and my heart was thudding. I sneaked a look at the messages:

'Get out here now or we're coming in.'

'Rape you and your mum.'

'NOW.'

Alarmed, I grabbed my coat and trainers and ran to the door.

"Where are you going?" Mum asked. "Look Christina, I don't want you going out every night 'til all hours. This all has to stop."

She stood in front of the door, barring my way, hands on her hips. With Pretos' threats ricocheting around my head, I lunged at her.

"Let me out!" I yelled. "I want to go. You don't understand!"

Mum stood firm and, without a conscious thought, I leaned in and bit her on the top of her arm. She yelped in pain and astonishment and loosened her hold on me. Shamefully, instead of stopping to see if she was alright, less still apologise, I took my chance and ran from the house. Just as he had threatened, Pretos was waiting further up the street with a car full of men.

"Here she is," he smiled. "Knew you'd see sense."

When I got home later, I found Mum with her head in her hands.

"I've reported the assault to the police," she told me tearfully. "It was the hardest thing I've ever done. But you need help. You need to change. And maybe this is the only way forward. I have tried everything else."

The police took a photo of Mum's bruise; a time-stamped and clinical reminder of my loss of control. This made it all so official. But I didn't need a photo. I knew the shame would live with me forever. I was interviewed with a solicitor present, and though Mum had pleaded with the police to be lenient on me, nobody could make me feel any worse than I already did. I blamed myself, and rightly so. This was yet another low. I seemed to have a capacity for outdoing myself in terms of bad behaviour.

Yet the police charges did little to shock me back to normality. If anything, I simply sank lower. I felt I had nothing left to lose. I got into fights and more robberies, all under the instruction of the gang.

One evening, I was out with one of the men and we had parked outside a fast-food restaurant. We noticed two teenage girls, who appeared worse for wear, at the side of the car and one tapped on to the window to ask the driver if he was a taxi.

"Sure," he smirked. "Jump in."

The girls got in the back seat and my heart sank. I knew full well what he was planning, and instead of driving them home, he took them to the nearest cashpoint.

"Get the money out, hand it over, and give me your phones," he ordered.

Bewildered, they did exactly as he said. As we drove away, leaving the girls on the pavement, I began tapping one hand frantically with the other. I felt so ashamed. It was a despicable and contemptible way to behave. This wasn't who I was – or was it? I had lost touch with the old Christina completely. I doubted she would ever come back. I was certain too that the girls would report us, they probably had the car make and registration, and they had our descriptions too. Sure enough, a few days later, I was arrested again. I was given bail, awaiting a court date for the burglary, the street robbery, and the assault on Mum. I had quite a list.

Incredibly, despite all the trouble I was causing, Mum and Dad took me out for a meal to celebrate my 18th birthday in August 2009.

"Happy birthday, pet," Dad beamed.

They showered me with love and affection, and waiting outside, on the street, was a little blue Micra.

"For you," Dad beamed.

He had already paid for driving lessons for me, and now I had my very own car.

"Thanks," I stuttered, bowled over by their generosity. But their kindness just made me feel even more abject and undeserving. My secret hung inside me like a dark, inaccessible mass. Still, I saw myself as the perpetrator and not the victim and I was terrified that my parents might reject me if they ever found out the extent of my lies or the details of my other life. I didn't fully understand that their love was unconditional and that no matter what I had done, or what I had not done, that would never change.

Pretos and the gang took me to Blackpool for my 18th birthday and it was the same tired routine; there was endless money to blow in the arcades and in the attractions. I had a great day, but on the way home, to balance the books, I was required to surrender my body to whoever wanted it. I knew better than to object when a hand started to slither up my leg, as I sat on the back seat of the car. This was all part of the package.

As part of my bail conditions, I was required to be home by 7pm, but Pretos didn't let that bother him at all, and it was late by the time we arrived back in Huddersfield. I made a big show of not being concerned myself either.

"Who cares?" I joked. "What are they gonna do about it anyway?"

The men laughed along with me.

I let myself in quietly, so as not to wake my parents, and lay awake almost the whole night. I was 18 now, officially an adult. It was the age when I was supposed to mature and look to the future with some clarity. And yet I was more disturbed and confused than ever. Who were these men? Friends or monsters? Sometimes, I wanted help. Often, I was scared. Occasionally, I understood that I was a victim. Mostly, I blamed myself. Sometimes, I loved being with the gang. Other times, I saw no way out and I thought I had no choice. I also realised I'd accepted, and continued to accept, drugs and alcohol and food from the gang and I did not know how to repay them, other than to do as they said. I was as dependent on Pretos and his men now, as I had been at 14. Even at 18, I simply could not move on.

* * * *

Late in 2010, I began to feel tired and nauseous. I had a nagging lower back ache, and I was weepy and moody. I had felt like this once before and I was sure, before I even bought the test, that I was pregnant. I had an on-off 'boyfriend', in the gang, but it clearly wasn't a serious relationship. If I had the baby, I'd be on my own.

I was very scared of becoming a mother but far more scared of having a termination. The memory of the abortion haunted me still, creeping into my dreams and plaguing my thoughts. I was tormented by so many layers of recriminations. If I'd had the baby, if I'd had my little Gracie, she would have been almost three years old by now. Toddling around, potty-trained, sleeping through the night, learning a new word every day. I'd see other children, the same age, and it tore me apart. Much as I accepted that I could not have raised a child back then, neither was I ready to say goodbye.

I knew I could not go through that again. I owed it to myself and to the baby I had lost. But I also had to face the prospect of my forthcoming criminal trial, set for February 2011. What kind of start was that, for me as a mother? What kind of start was that for my baby? How would I provide for us both? With a criminal record, I was unlikely to get a job. The problems were mounting. Even so, my mind was made up. We would face whatever the trial brought, and we would face it together. I went to see my parents, and they were both supportive of my decision. Mum had seen how badly the termination had affected me and she was keen to help me with this pregnancy.

"You'll be fine," she promised.

"We're here for you," Dad added. "You know that, pet. Always."

But after Christmas 2010, time seemed to accelerate, and

the spectre of the court date loomed before me. A couple of weeks beforehand, I had a scan which showed I was carrying a little boy. Seeing his little arms and legs wriggling on the monitor; gazing at his blurred but beautiful features, just melted my heart.

"Mummy's here," I whispered. "Can't wait to meet you."

All I wanted to do was buy baby clothes and paint a nursery and look forward to my new arrival. Instead, I had to plan for the trial. To be on the safe side, just in case I was jailed, Mum and I went out shopping, buying everything I needed. We came home laden with baby clothes, bedding, a cot, a pram and a car seat.

In February, as planned, I appeared at Bradford Crown Court charged with the assault on Mum, burglary, three counts of robbery and possession of an offensive weapon. I pleaded guilty to the lot. I saw no point in telling any more lies. I was done with all that.

"You need to prepare for a custodial sentence," my solicitor had warned. "Pack a bag when you come to court. You may well need it."

But for some reason, I had a very firm belief that I would not be jailed. By now, I was six months pregnant, and perhaps I thought the judge would take pity on my condition. Or maybe I was in complete denial, refusing to recognise how serious the situation was and how much damage I had caused. On the day of the sentencing, I arrived at the court in a white maternity shirt and black trousers – and without an overnight bag. I had with me just a bottle of fizzy orange juice.

Mum came to court with me, Dad was at work, which was for the best, because he was not cut out for the stress of the court hearing. He was so sensitive, and Mum was shielding him from much of what was happening. Besides, I was convinced I'd be home again later that day and I would see him then.

"You'll be okay," Mum told me, patting my hand. "You'll see."

When it was time for the sentencing, I was ordered to stand in the dock. In a daze, I listened as the judge sentenced me to three months for assault, 18 months for burglary, 18 months for one robbery, 18 months for the second, and two years for the third. There was no separate penalty given for possession of an offensive weapon. I was told I would serve a maximum of three-and-a-half years in a young offenders' institute.

Three-and-a-half years? I felt the world spinning around me. It just didn't seem real. My legs were buckling, my throat was tightening, and I reached out to grab my drink. But a security guard pulled my arm back sharply.

"You can't have that," she said. "You're going back down now."

My whole body was in the grip of a horrible, paralysing, fear. Instinctively, I cradled my bump, terrified of what lay ahead for us both. With tears streaming down my cheeks, I cast a panicky look at Mum. She was crying too.

I was taken back down to the cells where, because I was pregnant, I could not go in a van with the other prisoners, and so had to wait for a taxi to New Hall Young Offenders Institute in West Yorkshire. The journey passed in a blur. I stared blankly out of the window, nervously tapping my left hand with my right. I felt as though this was all happening to someone else. In another life, I was on my way home with Mum, chatting about cute baby clothes, preparing to carry out community service for my crimes. In the reception area, at the prison, I was booked in as prisoner A2168c. With the initial paperwork complete, I was told I could make one phone call.

"I'll ring my mum," I said tearfully.

But the moment she answered, the familiarity and tenderness in her voice, set against my alien and hostile setting, was too much for me. I burst into violent sobs and couldn't get a single word out. In the end, I had to hang up without even having spoken to her. After I calmed down, I was told to write out a list of numbers I might use whilst in prison, so that they could be approved by the security staff.

Afterwards, I was taken to a small room and made to strip completely, ready to be searched. I was even made to squat three times, so that the staff could check I was carrying nothing internally. I'd had no idea that this actually happened in real life. I'd thought that sort of thing was just for films.

"Really?" I asked, in a small, strangled voice. "I'm six months pregnant. Please don't make me squat."

It was demeaning, balancing my bump, completely naked, whilst I dropped down onto my knees. But there was no way out of it. At the hands of the gang, I'd suffered horrendous humiliation. And here in prison, it just seemed to go on and on. This was directed somehow at my baby, as well as me. I hated that he was involved, and I hated myself for involving him.

"I am so sorry," I whispered, my hands on my belly.

Because of my pregnancy, I was not allowed to share a cell, which I was quietly relieved about. I was taken instead to a single cell, upstairs on B wing. Inside was a single bed, with a toilet and sink next to it, separated by a curtain. There was also a small cabinet for my things. I had a plastic pillow and mattress and a standard issue green prison duvet. I swallowed down the lump in my throat. My Groovy Chick bedroom felt so very far away. My old life, my cat, my Rosie doll, all felt like they were on another planet; relics of a different age, distant echoes of a happier time. I remembered how Rosie had broken her arm, and how it had never really been the same after it was fixed at the doll hospital. And now, her hair was falling out. She was creaky and a little grubby and definitely past her best; a symbol of my lost childhood. She and I were broken; fractured and mangled. I was in pieces, and worse, I didn't know how to put myself back together. I thought of Rosie, lying on my old bed back at home, and I could almost taste the longing. I felt suffocated by my sorrow.

"You won't be allowed to keep your baby," said a prison officer, nodding at my bump as she stood at the cell door. "You have convictions for violence."

I was busy unpacking a few photos and her words lacerated through me, like a knife. I sank onto the squeaky mattress to catch my breath. This had never even occurred to me.

"Please don't take him away," I pleaded. "Please. I've learned my lesson. I got mixed up with a gang. I didn't have any choice, I had to do what they said. I had to do the robberies."

The officer listened and agreed to pass my request on to the authorities. But that seemed to make no difference. In floods of tears, at my next phone call, I relayed the news to Mum.

"Leave it with me," she replied. "I'll get some advice. See what we can do. But don't worry, even if you can't keep the baby, I will help you. He won't be taken away."

I tried not to dwell on it, I knew the stress wouldn't be good for my unborn son. I went through the motions each day; showers, mealtimes, exercise. But the risk of losing my baby eclipsed every other thought. The stress was crushing me, physically. At breakfast, I couldn't even lift my head properly.

"What's the matter?" asked one of the other girls. "You look fed up. You'll get used to it in here, love."

"I'm worried about my baby," I told her.

"It'll be alright, you'll see," she promised me. "Things have a way of working out."

I was grateful for her optimism, and I hoped it might even rub off on me. I had expected the other prisoners to be intimidating and aggressive, which wasn't the case. Everyone seemed friendly enough, though with a single cell, I didn't mix much. I wasn't permitted to have a job either, with the other girls, but was instead advised to sign up for some educational courses. The thought of going back to school did not fill me with enthusiasm but, with the months stretching ahead, empty and hollow, I realised I needed a way to fill the mind-numbing boredom of prison life. I signed up for a cleaning qualification, hoping that if nothing else it would act as a distraction.

"This might be useful for you, when you get out," said the teacher. "You could get yourself a job in cleaning."

I stared at her, uncertainly. I didn't ever see myself returning to the real world, getting a job, being a parent, rejoining society. I thought I didn't deserve those chances.

* * * *

As I got used to the schedule in prison, I became anxious about getting injured or bundled aside in the morning shower rush, and my baby being hurt. One morning, I got caught up in the crush, and it scared me. I spoke to a prison officer, and afterwards she arranged to let me use the shower block when everyone else was at work. It was such a relief to shower alone. Those few moments of privacy, knowing that me and my baby were safe, were invaluable to me.

"Thank you," I said gratefully, as the officer took me each day to the shower block.

She didn't have to go out of her way to help me. Those small acts of consideration meant a lot.

Two weeks on, a solicitor contacted the prison, and it was agreed that I would, after all, be allowed to keep my baby after he was born. In tears of gratitude and relief, I was moved to a mother and baby wing. Here, I was allocated a much nicer room with a separate toilet and sink, and a tiny cot inside too. Despite the environment, I felt a little rush of excitement when I saw the tiny little sheets and blankets. I imagined my baby lying there, smiling back at me, and I was filled with warmth and love. Despite everything, I had so much hope.

"Not long now, little one," I whispered.

On the new wing, I quickly adapted to yet another new routine. During the day, I was busy studying in class. Over the months, after my cleaning course was finished, I would go on to study food hygiene, health and safety and finally hairdressing. Each certificate of completion gave me a small sense of achievement; it was a step back in the right direction. Now, like many people who wasted their school years, I regretted not working harder. I saw this as my second chance. And I loved learning about hairdressing, I had a natural flair, and vowed, on the outside, to one day make this my career.

In the evenings, I'd ask the prison officers to lock my door after the evening meal, so that I could shut myself away and watch *Hollyoaks* on my own. I was quite happy, locked in my cell for the evening with my own thoughts. My parents visited every weekend, and my grandparents and cousins came occasionally too.

"You're doing really well," they told me. "And the baby is growing too. Your bump gets bigger every week!"

The visits were hardest, I think, for my dad. He and I would both hold back our tears as we faced each other across a rickety table, but as soon as I got back to my cell, I would break down. And I knew, without being told, that he would be just the same; allowing himself to cry only as soon as he got into the privacy of his own home. I missed him so much.

All of my antenatal appointments were conducted in prison so I had no reason to leave the unit. Each check went well and the pregnancy was progressing smoothly. The midwives were always ready with little snippets of advice and support for swollen ankles or stretch marks. They helped me to work out a birth plan and I had chosen Mum as my birthing partner.

"You're almost there, Christina," they smiled. "Your baby will be in your arms before you know it."

But my due date came – and went – and there was no sign of my baby boy. I longed for the contractions to start, but there was nothing.

"Not a single twinge!" I told the midwife.

"We will book you in for an induction," she told me. "Leave it with me."

But the days passed, and I didn't hear anything. I grew more and more frustrated.

"I need to be induced," I told the prison staff.

But they didn't know anything about it. Then, two weeks after my due date, I woke up from a nap to find my pyjamas were soaked. At first, I thought I had wet the bed, and I was mortified. I cleaned myself up quickly and asked if I could call my mother urgently. I was hoping she'd reassure me that this was perfectly normal.

"You haven't wet yourself, your waters have broken," Mum explained. "You need to tell a staff member. I will ask for permission to come to the hospital, and I will meet you there."

Though this was exactly what I had been hoping for, I was a jangle of nerves as I packed my bag. The arrangements for the journey seemed to take forever and it was 6pm when I arrived at the hospital. By now, I was yelling at the top of my voice.

"Where's my mum?" I wailed, as another contraction ripped through me.

I was told she was still awaiting clearance from the prison. Instead, two prison officers stayed with me in the delivery suite. In despair, I learned I was allowed only paracetamol as pain relief because my labour was too far advanced for anything stronger.

"I'm sorry, love," the midwife said. "You're going to have to manage with a couple of painkillers."

"What?" I gasped, biting down on the sleeve of my dressing gown. "You're joking!"

I was in agony. I was handcuffed to a prison officer too, all through my contractions. Each time I moved a little, I heard the clink of metal, a reminder I was giving birth in chains. I was uncomfortable enough without being bound to a total stranger. Yet I understood, even through the thick wall of pain, that there was nothing I could do about it.

One of the prison officers, an older lady, told me she was a mum and a gran herself, and she exuded such calm and confidence that I felt completely safe putting my trust in her. She held my hand and helped with my breathing and offered me sips of cold water.

"Breathe now," she instructed, checking the pattern of my contractions. "And now. You can ride the pain, Christina. You're doing fabulously.

"And breathe."

I focused on her, on her kind eyes, on the crinkles around them, each line no doubt with a story to tell.

As I reached full dilation, the midwife turned to the prison officers, and said firmly: "This girl should not be in handcuffs. She is about to give birth. Where is the humanity?"

I was in so much distress, I barely noticed as I was uncuffed. At 9.55pm, my beautiful son, Liam, was born, weighing 7lbs 7ozs. He was absolutely perfect.

"Welcome to the world, little one," I murmured, as I held him in my arms.

Just a few moments later, Mum and Dad burst into the room, carrying armfuls of clothes, teddies, and blankets. They had brought sandwiches and cakes and flasks of tea and coffee too.

"Oh love," Mum said. "We've been waiting for approval from the prison. I wasn't allowed to come without it.

"I'm so sorry I wasn't here for the birth."

Little Liam was by now finding his lungs and mewling like a kitten.

"Give him to me," Dad insisted, his face creased in two with the proudest beam. "Sure, he has swallowed the Blarney Stone, just like his mammy! He is going to be a little chatterbox!"

It was a lovely moment, the three generations, me, my parents and my son. Mum passed the sandwiches and drinks around the prison officers and the medical staff. Dad chatted away with the prison officer who had helped me to give birth.

"We'll always be grateful to you," he smiled.

Keen to show off his grandfatherly skills, he offered to put on Liam's first nappy, but when he fastened it and held Liam up for inspection, Mum and I burst out laughing.

"It's down by his knees, Dad," I pointed out. "I think you went wrong somewhere."

"Well, it's been a long time since I changed a nappy," he blushed.

But then Mum checked the packet.

"My fault," she giggled. "I bought size three nappies. He needs size one. Like we said, we're out of practice."

Dad was dispatched to buy the newborn size and Mum and I spent that time, suspended in a bubble of love, gazing, transfixed, at Liam. I sent visiting orders out for my grandparents and my cousins to visit him the following day.

"Oh, he's a cracker," they all said. "A little prince."

I spent two nights in hospital, in a wonderful cocoon of happiness. The prison officers had agreed not to handcuff me again and I felt sure that my parents had helped to win them over.

"We can trust you," smiled one of the officers. "We know you're not about to run for the hills."

After my stay in hospital, I went back to the mother and baby wing, along with my new son. I got on well enough with the other young mums, most were in prison for drug-related offences and, like me, were determined to use their time in jail to turn their lives around.

We settled into a new, hectic, yet joyous routine of feeding, sleeping, studying, and walking outside in the recreation area. On Sundays, I attended mass in the prison chapel. I hadn't been a church-goer before I was jailed, but now I found peacefulness and tranquillity in the chapel. Perhaps a part of me hoped I might find some redemption too.

13

Opening Up

It was not, of course, ideal, having my baby son in prison. There were moments when I felt overwhelmingly sad that I was not able to go out for long walks, to take him shopping, to make decisions for him, and, worse, that my parents and my wider family were missing out on those precious early days.

I was crippled with guilt – because as his mother, the one person who was supposed to protect him – I had let him down terribly. So many times, growing up, I had imagined becoming a mum pushing a pram, choosing little outfits. Never, ever, did I picture being a parent behind bars.

There were days when I got extremely frustrated with the minor details too. If I wanted to take a cute photo of Liam, to record a moment that I could share with my parents at visiting time, I had to ask a prison officer to do it for me. I was not allowed to have a camera or camera phone. And by the time I had found an officer, and they had agreed to my request, the moment had invariably passed.

So many memories drizzled away like that. I wasted so much time. I felt as though I was being punished, over and over, every day, and sometimes those smallest of penalties were the ones which caused me the most distress.

And yet, in other ways, prison was strangely a relief and a release to me. For whilst prison kept me in, it also kept the others out. And for the first time, since I was 14 years old, I felt absolutely safe. The groomers could not reach me here. Each night, I went to sleep, surrounded by violent and dangerous criminals. Yet perversely, when my door was locked, I knew that my boy and I were completely secure and away from harm. I didn't lie awake stressing about bricks through the living room window or threatening text messages on my phone. I wasn't coerced into having sex. I wasn't beaten up. I wasn't force-fed drugs. I had escaped it all. Deep down, I knew prison was not a long-term remedy. But it gave me peace of mind and provided solace for my injured soul.

With so much time on my hands, and spending so long each day alone, I reflected increasingly on the reasons I had been jailed. For the first time, I empathised genuinely with the people I had hurt; the lady whose bag I had stolen, Mum's friend who I had burgled, and of course, Mum herself. Only now, as the picture took shape and crystallised in my mind, did I begin to see how disgraceful and appalling my behaviour had been, towards completely innocent people.

I didn't want to think about the gang. I wanted to pretend they had never even existed. I had become expert at blocking them out, pushing them into a dusty corner of my brain where they would not be unearthed. Yet, when I slept, it was not so easy. Like snakes, they slithered out of their corner and slid into my dreams. I had horrible, technicolour nightmares, which flashed back over the abuse. Sometimes, I woke in the early hours, drenched with sweat and shaking with fear.

"What's wrong?" asked a night-shift officer, as I woke one morning. "I heard you crying out. You sounded really scared."

"Nothing," I mumbled. "I'm fine."

But as the weeks passed, the dreams became more vivid and more terrifying. I began to dread going to bed. I couldn't escape Pretos after all. Even in prison, he had found a way to get at me. The memories clung to me as though they were magnetised. I could not shake them off. The trauma, perversely, impacted me more now than it had during those years of daily abuse.

In one dream, I was in the front passenger seat and Pretos was driving with one hand on the wheel. He was pulling down my jeans with his other hand, and I was trying to fight him off, and wriggle free.

"Leave me alone!" I yelled.

But instead of hitting me, as I would have expected, Pretos just laughed and turned his attention to the person on the back seat.

"I can have her instead," he smirked.

I looked over my shoulder and saw to my horror that it was my mum on the back seat and she was his next victim. By refusing Pretos, I had landed it all on her.

"Sorry," I sobbed, through my sleep. "Sorry, Mum."

When I woke up, I was still crying. All day, the dream bothered me. Eventually, the prison officers suggested I should speak to the chaplain.

"We think it might do you good to talk about these night-mares," they explained. "You obviously have a lot on your mind. It could help to discuss this with the chaplain."

I was not sure, at first. I had met the chaplain at weekly mass and I liked her. But I didn't know if I'd be able, or willing, to articulate the exact source of my torment. In the end, the decision was made for me when the chaplain caught up with me after mass the following Sunday and offered me a coffee.

She was a warm lady, with short black hair held back with a headband. She wore an official collar and cassock but at the same time seemed very approachable and down-to-earth. I knew, just from her demeanour, that she would not make any judgements on me.

"I'm just here to listen," she told me. "Tell me what you like, there is no pressure."

"So," I began. "It started at the bus station. I was skipping school because I was being bullied…"

At first, the conversation was stilted, and I purposely steered away from anything connected with the abuse. I focused on being overweight, on the bullies, and on those early fun times we had, playing truant.

But then, the chaplain began asking me direct questions about my convictions.

"Why did you attack your mum?" she asked me. "And why did you burgle your mum's friend? You don't seem like that sort of girl at all to me."

I stared at my hands, my cheeks hot with humiliation.

"I'm not," I said earnestly. "Really. Please don't think that of me. I did it because I had no choice."

And with that, it all tumbled out. It was as though I'd wrenched the lid off a pressure cooker and a torrent of steam followed. I told her everything I could, right from that first rape, when I had barely been conscious. Breathless, like a car without brakes, I told her about the 'parties', the vodka, the cannabis, the pills, the stomach-churning and unavoidable physical, sexual and mental assaults which had formed the spiky bedrock of my daily life. I remembered the terrifying attacks on my family home, the threats to me and to my parents. I explained how I was forced to commit crimes just as I was forced to perform oral and full sex.

In the incongruous surroundings of a Catholic chapel, with the holy statues staring back at me, I told her how the gang used plastic bags as condoms. How we were forced to have sex with strange men, usually more than one, often with an audience, sometimes recorded on film. The memories rushed to the surface as though they had been bursting for a whiff of oxygen. But each one brought with it unimaginable pain, and the shame burned right through me like a blowtorch.

"Christina, this was not your fault," the chaplain said gently. "None of it was your fault. You are a victim."

I stared at her, not really taking it in. I thought I had misunderstood.

"How?" I asked eventually. "Surely most of it was my fault? I went out to meet them each night. I could have said no, but I was too scared. I could have stayed at home, but I didn't.

"This all started with me playing truant. I brought it all on myself."

"Christina, you were a child," she replied. "None of this is down to you. Have you heard of grooming gangs? Do you understand what CSE means? Child sexual exploitation?"

I shook my head.

"I know I promised to listen only," she said. "But this is so serious. I'd like you to report this to the police. This needs to be investigated."

I frowned at her.

"I really don't think there is any point in that," I said. "My parents called the police so many times when I was out with the gang. They said there was nothing they could do.

"They seemed to think it was my fault because I kept going back to them."

But the chaplain shook her head and insisted.

"I would like you to tell them what you have told me," she said. "Please."

And in that moment, there was a slight chip into the armour I had built up around myself. I felt myself softening and relaxing. Here was someone – someone kind and caring who I trusted completely – telling me that the abuse was not my fault.

"Really?" I whispered. "You think so?"

I wasn't a tactile person – not since the abuse had started – but I wanted to hug her. I wanted to show how much it meant, just for someone to see me, to really see me, and to hear my voice. She was the first person to ever believe me. The first person to listen to my story. Words would never be enough to show her how grateful I was.

"I'll speak to the police," I agreed. "As long as you can be with me."

Walking out of the chapel, I felt a little lighter, a little stronger, and a little less alone. I wasn't sure I really believed that I was a victim in all of this. But I was willing to see where this took me.

Mum was called to the prison the following week, and I told her most of what I had told the chaplain. She visibly winced and her tears flowed as I confided the details of the abuse. But I could not bring myself to tell her the worst of it. She was my mother, after all.

"I suspected something for a long time, but nothing as bad as this," she confessed. "I knew you were hiding a lot from us. But I began to think you had an older boyfriend and that you were mixed up with a gang of some sort.

"I never for a minute imagined you were being exploited. These men are animals, Christina. They have to be brought to justice."

"I thought you'd be annoyed with me," I wept. "I kept it to myself for so long because I was convinced I'd get into trouble.

"I had to keep going out there, and doing as they said, because I thought they would kill me or they would even kill you and Dad. Remember the loose wheels? The broken windows? The funeral wreath on our doorstep? That was all the gang.

"All those phone calls, the threats, the abuse. It was all them. I had no choice. I had to do as they said."

Mum was distraught. Now, as a mother myself, I could

finally see how horrific this must be for her, hearing details of how her little girl had been systematically and cruelly destroyed. No parent wants to hear that their child has been hurt. Mum had to listen to details of how I had been raped – and gang raped – over and over again. And it was then – and only then – that I could say this out loud. I didn't want the label. It made me feel dirty and ashamed. But slowly, very slowly, I felt a stirring inside me; the germination of a journey which would end in understanding and acceptance. I allowed myself to consider the idea that I had been abused and raped and groomed and exploited. Tentatively, I examined the possibility that I was a victim.

My meetings with the chaplain, and with my mum, were hugely cathartic. I questioned everything that had happened to me, since meeting the gang. I saw my past through a new lens, and the picture it threw back at me was completely different to the one I had believed for so long. Could it be that I was not in the wrong after all?

But the meetings also opened up a locked box inside my head and more memories, harsh and loathsome, crawled out like cockroaches.

'That's for showing me up in front of my boys…'

'You little slag. Get out. You can walk home…'

'Hey guys, Tina raped me and she loved it…'

In June 2011, a male police officer in plain clothes came to the prison. It was arranged that I would speak to him, in the privacy of the chapel, with the chaplain present. Again, the setting seemed slightly unreal; I felt the eyes of the statues upon me; critical or supportive? I could not yet tell. The candles flickered on the altar, and, as I began to speak, I felt that the air was thick with judgement, because yes, I felt judged. Not by the church. Not by the chaplain. Not by the police. Not even by the statues. But by myself. No matter how much I tried to convince myself that this was not my fault, the doubts crept back in, like spiders.

I told the officer everything I could remember, though much of the detail of the past five years had blurred into one. There had been so many parties, my consciousness fuddled by alcohol and drugs, that it was impossible to distinguish one from the next. But I tried to explain that I had carried out the robberies and the attacks under duress, for the same reasons I'd had sex and performed sex acts. That I was too frightened to say no. That I had feared for my life, my parents' lives. That I was incapable of making a decision for myself. That Christina O'Connor was lost to me, stolen away, and I didn't know how to get her back. The officer took notes, asked questions, and promised to investigate and come back to me.

"Thanks for talking to me," he said, as he closed his notebook. "I appreciate it can't have been easy."

He went away and I felt a growing faith in him. I really believed this might be the start of something. And over the weeks which followed, the chaplain often asked me if I had heard anything from the police.

"No," I told her. "Nothing at all."

More time passed.

"Nothing," I told her again. "Not even a phone call."

I could tell she was disappointed. But I had no regrets. I

would remember her always as my turning point and my catalyst for change. Prison was my punishment. But prison was also my salvation.

* * * *

Whilst we waited for news from the police, I concentrated on being the best mother I could to Liam. Because I had broken the conditions of my bail, after staying late in Blackpool with the gang for my 18th birthday, I had a blemish on my record. I was told I might have to serve my full sentence. Ruefully, I remembered how I had scoffed at the law when I had arrived back late that evening. Well, I was certainly paying for that now. I had grown up and matured in prison. I had become a parent, I had atoned for my crimes, and I saw now how crass and fatuous my behaviour had been.

Determined to put it behind me, I did my best to show the authorities that I had changed. I tried hard to be a model prisoner. And in time, due to the progress I made, I was moved to an open prison in York, and then I was informed that I would be allowed to have a home visit.

"What? Me and Liam? Back to Huddersfield?" I asked incredulously.

Though I had known the announcement was coming, it took me by surprise. And it was a bittersweet privilege too, because as much as I was looking forward to seeing my family and taking Liam home, I was wary of bumping into the gang. And now that my parents had some idea of the extent of their wickedness, they were concerned too.

"We need to think of Liam," they told me. "What if they target him?"

I shrugged helplessly. I felt like I had an axe, constantly hanging over my neck. It seemed I would never be free.

"I'm not hiding away at home," I said fiercely. "I'm not being ruled by them. Not any more."

But although I was talking a good game, I didn't feel as brave as I sounded, and my parents knew it. I had the added worry that, by now, as a result of my police interview, Pretos and the others might well have been arrested and questioned. If they knew I'd made a police complaint, they would be out for revenge. And I dreaded to think what form that might take.

My first trip home, despite all the stress, was lovely. I couldn't wait to show Liam off to my family and my neighbours. And just being inside a bedroom – and not a cell – was wonderful. The change was so subtle; each room had a bed, a cabinet, a cot. Yet that subtlety was everything. Back in the comforting folds of my family, I began to feel once again like Christina; a person with a name, and not simply Prisoner A2168c.

One Saturday afternoon, on another home visit, I was out pushing the pram when I spotted a dark-coloured Honda coming towards me, braking quite sharply. As it drew nearer, my heart started to race. Pretos was driving, with another of the men in the passenger seat. On the back seat were three girls who looked so young – so heartbreakingly young – and yet, I realised with a jolt, they were probably the same age as I was when I'd first met the gang.

Pretos opened his window, and I fixed my face into a smile.

"Okay?" I asked hopefully.

I tried to sound casual, but my mind was in overdrive. I wondered whether the police had spoken to them. I worried that they might expect me to go back working for them. To simply pick up where I had left off.

"You out?" Pretos asked.

"No," I said, shaking my head. "Just weekend leave. I won't be here long."

He leered into the pram.

"New car?" I asked, to distract him away from Liam, but he ignored me.

"So this is your kid?" he said.

I felt a shiver run right through me. I didn't dare object. But I didn't want him within a mile of my beloved son.

"I need to get back," I said eventually. "He needs his bottle, you know. Babies are hard work."

The next day, when it was time to go back to prison, Mum and Dad were distraught, cuddling me and Liam and wishing we could stay.

"We miss you both so much," they said.

But in a way that I couldn't ever admit, I was looking forward to putting as many miles and as many walls between me and the gang as possible. In prison, I knew I was safe and part of me just wanted to get back there and stay there. It wasn't real life in prison, I knew that. But I'd had enough of real life. I felt it was vastly overrated. Besides, I was of the firm belief that prison had actually saved my life. My sentencing, which had once felt like a grenade flung into my lap, was actually the greatest gift.

14

Digging the Past

A few weeks after Liam turned one, I was released early for good behaviour. I had served 15 months in total. I felt very conflicted and disorientated as I packed our things and said my goodbyes. I wanted to go home; sure I did. But I didn't want the hassle or the risk that came with it. Before I left, I made sure I saved a special farewell for the chaplain. Even though we had still heard nothing from the police, I knew I owed her everything.

"I will never forget you," I told her.

Mum and Dad turned up at the gates in the family Mondeo, and I rushed out to meet them with Liam in my arms.

"I can't believe you're coming home," Dad smiled. "Both of you."

Sleeping in my old bed, with Liam's cot slotted in tightly at the side, I felt as though I was on rewind. I was back to being a child, a scared, lonely child. Only this time, I had a child of my own too.

"Did you sleep alright?" Dad asked the following morning. "We've planned a little birthday party for Liam today. I know it's late but we ought to celebrate."

I knew they meant well. But the word 'party' brought me out in a cold sweat. And the thought of a gathering, with all my relatives in attendance, felt like an impossible over-facing. I just wasn't ready for it. Instead of enjoying the freedom of my family home, it felt too big, too open, too exposed. I didn't feel safe. I was used to my own little space, just me and Liam, and nobody else. I was used to locks on the doors and windows and guards on every exit. And, whilst that was limiting it was also strangely comforting. I missed it.

When the guests started to arrive, bringing presents and cakes and bottles of wine, I was overwhelmed. It was all so noisy and busy. I just couldn't cope with it, and I escaped to the seclusion and privacy of my bedroom.

"You'll get used to it," Dad reassured me, poking his head round the door. "It's a big adjustment, pet. We understand that."

* * * *

But as the days passed, I only felt worse. I was on a tag, so that I could be electrically monitored, and I was not allowed to leave the house after 7pm. Mum didn't like me to smoke indoors and so I had to have a cigarette out of the back door. Ludicrously, I had one leg in the house, to make sure I didn't break my licence conditions, and one leg out, so that I didn't blow smoke into the rooms. I felt as though the house itself was mocking me.

"This is ridiculous," I complained.

And though the house felt too big and too open, my little

bedroom suddenly felt suffocatingly small and tight. I felt as though the walls were marching in towards me, like a slow-moving army. I needed to get out. My predictable, dependable home life, which once had been soothing, was now stifling me and I could not breathe.

Life here, after my 15 months in a large and chaotic prison, seemed mind-numbingly dull and pedestrian. Nothing happened, day after day. It was the same routine, copy and paste, copy and paste, far worse than it had been at Newhall. Ironically, I felt more of a prisoner in my own home than I ever had in prison.

I can appreciate, with hindsight, that I was probably picking fault in everything. I complained that the house was too big, but it was also too small. I was bored at home, and yet I felt overwhelmed by visitors. I hated being stuck at home in the evenings even though I had been used to spending many hours locked in a cell. My problems ran deeper than my surroundings and deeper, too, than the surface tension between me and my parents, which was getting worse as each day went by.

Mum and I rowed over almost every minute detail. Again, looking back, I can see how unreasonable I must have seemed. She and Dad were supporting me; emotionally, practically and financially. Mum was just doing her best, helping out with Liam, giving me grandmotherly advice and tips. But I already suffered from a crippling lack of confidence, and I felt as if she was taking over.

"No, don't bath him now, he'll catch a cold."

"Don't hold him like that, you'll never get his wind up."

"You need to get him in a proper routine."

She meant well. But all I heard, refracted through a self-critical lens, was judgement and complaint. I started to believe that I was no good as a mother, just as I was no good as a daughter. I asked myself if Liam would be better off without me. Even at happy times, when he learned a new word, or he got a new pair of Wellington boots, I found it hard to smile.

"Mumma!" he beamed. "Mumma!"

I loved to hear him say it. But at the same time, if I was brutally honest with myself, I felt numb inside, as though my feelings had been cauterized at the nerve ends. My emotions were shrivelled and dead.

I tried taking Liam out for daytime walks, to escape the strain at home. But then, I was always on edge about bumping into one of the gang members. It was over a year now since I'd made my police complaint, and I'd heard nothing since. Despite the kindness of the chaplain, I had reverted to blaming myself again for what had happened. And the fact that the police had not taken my complaint further – and had not even seen fit to call me – only reinforced that. Clearly, I was in the wrong. I had to be. Why else would the police dismiss my complaint so readily?

Each time I saw Pretos, or one of the other men, on my walks, my throat would squeeze tight with fear. I felt so protective towards Liam, so worried that they might harm him, and it made me physically ill. I felt as though I might pass out with the stress. I took great care not to do anything to upset Pretos, nothing to make him retaliate.

"Hi," I'd say. "It's good to see you, all of you."

Pretos would always make an elaborate show of checking under the pram hood to look at Liam and it curdled my blood. Internally, I was screaming at him to back off. But on the outside, I simply smiled. On the outside, I knew better.

Strangely, he never once mentioned me going back to work for him, he never invited me to any parties and he never told me I had to have sex with any of his mates. There were no drugs or drinks on offer. He didn't even offer me a lift. It was as though none of it had ever happened. It all belonged to a past life and there was no overlap.

Yet still, I worried. And even though the conversation was polite, if a little awkward, there was always that undercurrent of fear and panic. In my mind's eye, I would envisage the men bundling me into the back of the car and letting Liam roll down the hill in his pram. Or I'd imagine them demanding that I hand him over, in exchange for some old and mythical drug debt. My mind ran riot with different scenarios. I knew from bitter experience they were capable of pretty much anything.

But incredibly, the days passed, and nothing happened. I'd see Pretos and the others for a quick chat, and then they'd drive off. I was wrong-footed by their new approach, always worrying they were planning something big; a kidnap, an assault, an attack on my home or my baby. I could not accept I would simply be allowed to walk away from their cult.

It wasn't until much later, as I looked back at those meetings, that I finally realised why I was no longer of interest to the gang. Luckily for me, but sickeningly for society, they didn't want me because I was too old. I was a mother now. I was an adult. I had lost my appeal. These men were paedophiles and I was no longer a child. I had outgrown my purpose.

Eight weeks on, when my tag was removed, I moved into a rented place, around a 15-minute walk from my parents' house. I knew I had to leave home, if nothing else to try to salvage the relationship with my mother. Dad and I never really argued, but she and I were clashing far too much, and we each needed some space.

Even in my new place, she and Dad were still very supportive, as they always had been. Dad helped me with the rent and the deposit, and he brought me bits of furniture and baby equipment.

"This is a new start," I told him, my eyes shining. "I want to make a go of things."

I enrolled at college to study Level Two Hairdressing, I had completed Level One in prison, and loved it. I got some work experience too, and I found a nice nursery for Liam nearby. At first, I was contented, or I told myself that I was. This was just what I had wanted; independence, space to breathe, room to be myself.

But annoyingly, I still felt something was missing. I had been away for so long and I struggled to settle into any kind of new routine. The abuse, and everything that went with it, felt like it had happened in another dimension. And that part of me felt like another girl. There was an uneasy gap, a gaping hole, in my mind, between the two existences. And though I tried to ignore it, it only seemed to get wider, and it hurt me and troubled me more.

Still, I persevered, knowing I owed it to Liam to make the best of our new situation. And living apart, Mum and I got on so much better and our relationship improved a little. I'd had no word from the police, and I had given up any hope of justice or redemption. I was angry with myself for trusting the officer, for allowing myself to pour out all of my darkest secrets to a stranger, who had then completely ignored me. I felt well and truly cancelled.

"It was your own fault," I told myself. "Put it behind you."

And so I scooped up all the memories which had spilled out in prison, and I packaged them away again, as though I was zipping a tent tightly into a bag. The abuse had started eight years ago. It was firmly in the past. And it would stay in the past. For good.

At the end of my college course, I got an apprenticeship in a hairdressing salon nearby. I was a customer there, off and on, and I knew the boss well. The salon was only two streets from my home, and it felt familiar and safe. It was just what I needed. I couldn't wait to start work, and, as I had hoped, I thrived there. At first, I was tasked with washing and blow-drying hair and mixing colours. As my skills improved, I progressed onto cutting and styling.

Hairdressing was perfect for me and the job gave me structure and routine and a sense of purpose. It also provided me with a wage. And I loved to ask my clients questions and hear all about their lives. I was perfectly happy to listen to them all day, just as long as I didn't have to talk about myself.

****

That brings me back to the day in July 2013 when that shock phone call from nowhere changed the course of my life.

"Christina O'Connor? Police child safe-guarding team here. I wondered if we could have a chat about what happened to you as a teenager?"

After recovering my composure, I had returned to the salon but the rest of the day passed in a blur of hair pins and hair spray.

"Can I have a few more curls around my face?"

"Those pins are digging in my head."

"Ooh, I hope the sun comes out. I can't wait to get that first glass of bubbly down me."

I nodded in mute reply to each exclamation. The excitement of the wedding party, their giggly hysteria and their jittery nerves, all sat in stark juxtaposition to my own silent despair. I could not speak. My mouth felt like it was full of dust. It was as though I was choking. Inside, my brain was churning, protesting silently, at this horrific and uninvited intrusion into my day.

'Child safeguarding team here!'

She had phoned me, out of the blue, all these years later, as though she was offering me a dental check-up. I had been unceremoniously dumped by the police, time and time again. My trust in them had been eroded over the years until there was now nothing left but an old wound. How dare they just rip off the scab and ring me, without so much as a warning? How did they even have my phone number? My fear was gradually mutating into anger and indignation.

"Everything okay?" asked my boss.

"Yeah fine," I replied abruptly. "Fine."

I was stuck inside my head. I couldn't let anyone else in. As soon as my shift was done, I went straight to see my parents.

"The cheek of it," Dad fumed. "The police have spent years ignoring us. Why now?"

"I know," I agreed. "I have no idea why they have suddenly contacted me after all this time. It really floored me, it came out of nowhere, I was working, I was on my way home to find some hair pins for a wedding party and my phone rang. I just couldn't take what she was saying to me. Anyway, I told her there is no way I am helping them. They can forget it."

My parents both jumped up in protest.

"Christina, you need to talk to the police," Mum insisted. "I know they've let you down in the past. But this is your chance to put these monsters in jail. They watched you serve a prison sentence yourself, knowing they forced you to commit those crimes. They were the ones who should have been convicted.

"They nearly ruined you. They nearly ruined our entire family. You can't let them get away with it."

I shook my head.

"It's too late," I said firmly. "I can't rake it all up again. I can't face it."

"If you won't do it for yourself, do it for all the other kids out there," Mum persuaded me. "You have a child, you have younger cousins. You told me yourself you had seen teenage girls in the back of the gang's cars.

"You have to speak out, for their sake, if not for yours."

There was a silence. And in a heartbeat, I saw, in my mind's eye, a ghostly image of a little girl with rosy cheeks and long brown hair – an image of the daughter I would have had, if the termination hadn't gone ahead. My little Gracie. Since then, I'd felt crippled, at times paralysed, by the guilt of the abortion. This was my chance now, not to put it right, but to do something right. It was a way of laying down a legacy for her. In her memory, in her name, I could speak out. It was too late to save my baby. It was not too late to save others.

I knew I had to do exactly as Mum said. The thought of anyone harming my child – or any other child – was unthinkable. There was a possibility, a mere glimmer of a chance, that something positive could come from my childhood ordeal and the loss of my unborn child. And if another young girl could be saved, thanks to me speaking out, it would surely ease my own agony too. Could I really turn this daily pain into a purpose? I realised I had no choice. I had to try. I had to speak to the police.

"Okay," I sighed. "Okay, I'll give it a go. I'll listen to what she has to say. No promises."

With a crackle of resentment, I called the number back, and two police officers, Samantha and Andrea, came to see me at home that same evening. That first visit was just for a chat. I knew this was an ice-breaker and they were eager to gain my trust. But I wasn't sure if, or how, to open myself up, yet again, for disappointment.

"What happened to my first statement?" I asked. "And why now? Why contact me, after years of silence?"

"I'm going to be completely honest with you," said one of the officers. "Your police statement, that you made in prison, was found down the back of a filing cabinet."

Her words clanged to the ground between us. There was a silence as I digested exactly what that meant.

"My statement was just… lost? Lost!" I spluttered eventually. "Shoved at the back of a drawer? Have you any idea how difficult it was for me to speak to the police back then?"

Apparently, more girls had come forward to make complaints and it was only now that my own account had been pulled out and dusted off. I was seething. "We'll give you time to think this over," Andrea said. "Let's meet up again soon."

I knew none of this was their fault. They were very professional, and they seemed genuine and caring. But I felt so let down. It had been unspeakably harrowing for me to make my statement in the prison chapel. I had shared something so personal, so traumatic, with the police officer. Yet for reasons I would never understand or accept, the statement had simply been shoved down the back of a drawer. Had anyone even bothered to read it before now? This felt like a further twist of the knife, it was more confirmation that I did not matter, that I was worthless, I was hopeless, and I was the one at fault.

"Lost!" I growled again, as I closed the front door and they drove away.

Over the next few months, the two police officers slowly built up a relationship with me and gradually, I began to confide in them. At first, we talked at my parents' home and I grew more comfortable around them.

"Do you feel ready to give a formal interview?" they asked.

I nodded. In March 2015, I underwent my first formal interview at Holmfirth Police Station. I knew that other girls, once my close allies, had made police complaints also. But Pretos had made sure he had turned us all against each other, over the years, and I counted none of them as friends now. I wanted no connection with anyone from my past, no matter whether they were perpetrator or victim.

In the interview, the officers showed me videos of the 'parties', taken from the phones of some of the gang members.

"Do you recognise anyone on these clips?" asked one of the officers.

As I looked at the images, I was transported back in time to those grotty houses, thick with smoke, rancid with depravity. The fear was like a pebble, jammed in my throat. And yes, I was immediately recognisable, in my favourite Kerry football shirt. I was there with some of the other girls. The footage was a little grainy, but I was moved by how young I looked. Just a clueless child.

"That's me," I pointed. "In the green and yellow football shirt."

"Do you still have the shirt?" they asked. "We'd like to send it for forensic testing."

I nodded. It was a special edition shirt and I had once loved it. I could not throw it away, despite the abhorrent memories attached to it.

"I can find it for you later," I offered.

What I didn't know was that the police would hand it back to me, months later, with sections chopped out of it. Dad was aghast; he had bought me the shirt and loved it almost as much as I did. Now my treasured possession was in pieces, reminiscent of the way I felt about myself. Both ruined, both beyond repair.

* * * *

A second interview took place in August 2015. I was struggling with times, dates and places and the officers arranged to drive me around the town, to try to jog my memory and firm up the timeline of the abuse. "Okay," I agreed.

I was not relishing the prospect, but I could see it might be helpful. We drove to the park, snooker hall and the reservoir. We continued alongside the canal, the taxi rank, the takeaways. We went as far as the moors and the dams and the water treatment plant. It was a bizarre experience; many of these locations were not particularly out of the way and I had driven past them myself several times. But now, in the context of the investigation, they took on a new and malevolent aspect. I felt myself pinned back against the passenger seat, immobilised with terror, unable to shake off the memories.

'U fancy being left here all on your own?'

'Do as I say or you get a slap.'

'See this knife? You get it if you backchat me again.'

As we parked at each place, I saw, in my mind's eye, the ghost of a little girl, crying and scared and all alone. I wanted to reach out to her, put my arms around her, and tell her she was going to be alright. But then, I wasn't sure if that was true. Would I ever be alright? Nobody could make that promise.

"You're doing well, Christina," the officers told me. "Just take it slowly."

Up on the moors, I had to battle against a panic attack, as I remembered Pretos threatening to leave me there on my own. And at the reservoir, where I had been brutally raped, more than once, I was physically sick. It was deeply traumatising, physically visiting the past in this way and forcing myself to relive it. But it was effective too, and slowly, more and more memories trickled back. I felt like Scrooge, on Christmas Eve, flying through the air with the Ghost of Christmas Past. Could this be my key to a better, redemptive life, a new start, as it had been for him?

Identifying the gang members was very tough too. They had all used those strange and sinister nicknames and I had never known their real names. I would never have dared to ask. Using photos, and footage, we were able to match up lists of names and nicknames with images, and I identified 11 of my abusers in total. There were many, many more. Others, I had to accept, would remain forever anonymous, forever unpunished.

The interviews, the identifications, the visits to the locations, were all part of a painstaking and gruelling process. By digging into the past, I felt as though I was pulling off a bandage, gouging out a wound and ripping out my own flesh. This felt self-destructive, like a form of self-harm. As yet, I saw no healing and no catharsis. But I hoped perhaps that lay ahead.

The abuse began to dominate my thoughts, both awake and asleep. Folding back the shutters in my mind which had protected me for so long, I relived many of the rapes and the assaults. Each night, lying in bed, on my own, I rewound back to the reservoir, to the park, to the water treatment plant. I remembered how I was summoned from my desk in lessons and ordered to perform the most horrific of sex acts, still in my uniform, still with my school bag by my side.

I had locked the abuse away so effectively but now, like an upturned box of beetles, my memories had been emptied all over the floor. And I could not gather them back in. It was as though I had fallen through a large sinkhole and landed back in 2005.

For weeks, I fought against the urge to drown out my fears with alcohol. But I had known, possibly from the start, that this was not a battle I could win, and I began drinking heavily. It was the only way I could blot out the torment. If Liam was staying with my parents, as he often was, I'd finish off a half-bottle of vodka a night to myself. If he was with me, I'd tuck him into bed and then take a stiff double vodka into my own bed and cry myself to sleep. But no matter how much I drank, Pretos plagued my dreams like a vengeful devil, eyes glowing, lips drooling.

"Your feet!" he ordered. "Show me your feet!"

But in the dream, my fingers had all morphed into useless blocks, and the more I fumbled with my laces, the tighter the knots became.

"I'm going as fast as I can!" I promised. "Doing my best."

Pretos stood over me, waving a baseball bat in his hand.

"Now!" he bawled. "Now!"

As the bat crashed with force onto my skull, I suddenly

awoke, cold with sweat and my heart thrashing against my chest. It took me a few moments to steady my ragged breathing.

"You're safe," I reminded myself. "It was just a dream."

But deep down, I wondered if I would ever be safe. I couldn't believe I'd had that life and done those things. The stigma was as raw now as it had been at that first party, that first rape, that first loss of innocence.

After months of turmoil and soul-searching, my statement was finally completed. I was handed a final copy to be signed and then passed on as part of the preparations for a forthcoming trial. I was warned that the men would soon be charged and, in time, would face judgement through the courts. The mere thought of seeing them in court left me paralysed with dread. I could not look ahead to the future. It took all of my strength and willpower simply to make it through each day.

15

Hours to Live

During those evenings, I rarely left my home. I found it stressful enough going about my day-to-day errands. Even going to work or popping into the supermarket felt like a calculated risk. Several times, when I had been collecting Liam from the nursery, I had caught sight of Pretos or the other men parked at the side of the street. Though they never even spoke to me, I felt exposed and intimidated. The threat was always there, hanging in the air, like a bad odour that would not go away.

One night, I was invited to a 21st birthday celebration and my parents persuaded me to go.

"You never go out," Dad said. "We'll babysit for you. It will do you good to enjoy yourself."

Reluctantly, I agreed. And I had to admit, it was nice to see all the old faces again and catch up with friends from years ago. It was only a short walk home, and though it was late, I decided to chance it. But, as I hurried along, I heard a car slowing behind me and a fear settled on me like ice.

"Hey!" shouted a voice I knew well. "White bitch! Get in this fucking car now!"

I broke into a run in my high heels, but I heard a car door slamming and then a hand grabbed my hair and yanked me back.

"You're a dirty white prostitute," spat Pretos. "That's what you are."

There were several men, all kicking and punching me, as I lay on the pavement. It was only when other cars began to slow down that they fled. For a few moments afterwards, I lay, curled in a foetal ball, my whole body racked with sobs. My dress was ripped, and my make-up was smudged with tears. I limped home and even though I locked and double-locked every door and window, I felt so vulnerable. I didn't believe this was ever going to stop.

I knew the gang members had probably been arrested and interviewed by now and the attack on me was doubtless in retaliation. The idea of facing them in court seemed unthinkable. This would only get worse and worse as the months passed.

"I just can't do it," I sobbed, as I climbed into bed, a bottle of vodka in my hand.

I had managed to leave the gang behind. I had spoken to the police about the abuse. I had finally done the right thing. Yet in many ways, I was still trapped. They still controlled me and bullied me. I wanted to leave Huddersfield and I wanted to run away from my past. Yet I didn't want to leave my family. Neither did I have the confidence to start again elsewhere. It was all such a mess. I was referred to mental health services, and prescribed medication. But this wasn't a solution; it was no more than a sticking plaster on a gaping laceration, gushing blood, leaving me too injured and too weak to carry on.

One night, in the depths of despair, I took an overdose of my medication. Counting out the pills, I felt it would be better for everyone if I wasn't here. Later that night, my parents became concerned when I didn't reply to their messages, and they called the police. I was rushed to hospital to have my stomach pumped.

"I'm sorry," I wept. "I didn't mean to cause you all this trouble."

Even at my very lowest, especially at my very lowest, I saw everything as my fault. I couldn't grasp the concept that I was not to blame.

On another occasion, I wandered, almost in a trance, to the local train station. On the platform, with my blood rushing through my veins, I waited for the fast train to come. I had every intention of throwing myself onto the track and underneath the wheels.

"You can do it," I whispered to myself. "This is the best way."

I just couldn't take any more. I was so ashamed of who I was and what I had done. I hated being myself.

My cousin, Martin, knew I'd been feeling depressed, and, as I waited for the train, he called me to see how I was. I didn't have the strength to tell him a lie.

"I'm done," I replied. "Done with everything."

"You have to listen to me," he said firmly. "Put your big girl pants on. Walk away from the station. I am coming to meet you."

I did as he said, simply because I didn't know what else to do. I credited him with saving my life that night, and many other times too. When my moods slid into thoughts of self-harm and suicide, I tried to focus on the kindness of my cousin, on the devotion of my parents, on my love for my son. But the negative voices and the memories of the abuse were always somehow louder and more insistent, drowning out the others. I attempted suicide again and again, unable to see a way forward.

Late one night, I climbed onto a bridge, overlooking the M62 motorway, and spent hours staring down at the traffic thundering past. As I tried to pluck up the courage to jump, I began flicking through my phone, looking at photos of my beloved family, and slowly my resolve began to crack and waver. I realised, desperate as I was, I could not leave them.

And yet, on another day, when flashbacks of the abuse flooded my mind like sewage, I vowed to end my life again. This time, I swallowed some of Dad's medication and I made my way to our local cricket club. I knew I could drop down onto the railway tracks from a ledge behind the cricket pitch and throw myself underneath an on-rushing train. Luckily, I was spotted by friends who alerted my family, and they took me home.

"Please, pet, stop doing this," Dad begged. "We don't want to lose you."

I am still unsure whether each of these episodes was a cry for help or a genuine attempt at suicide. Probably, I think, they were a frenzied mixture of both. I did not want to live. Yet neither did I want to die.

My solution, the only one I had ever known, was to drink more. I was late for work a few times. Once or twice, I just didn't show up at all. I had gone from loving my job to absolutely dreading going to work. I couldn't face my boss, or the customers. I was no longer fit for the role and in January 2016, I lost my job.

"You're just too hit and miss," my boss said.

I couldn't blame her. I was becoming a liability. And I was feeling increasingly sorry for myself too. If I'd had a visible illness, or a recognised condition, people around me would have shown me sympathy and patience. But because of my acute sense of shame, I kept my problems secret. Nobody, outside my close family, knew about the grooming gang and the police investigation. Nobody understood why I behaved so erratically. Ironically, speaking to the police about my past had stirred up all my old anxieties and left me so I could not confide in anyone else. I could not share my burden again. People presumed I was just a heavy drinker, a flaky friend, an unreliable worker. It went no deeper than that.

And so, inadvertently, the gang got what they wanted. As they always did. I kept my mouth shut about the abuse, just as they had always demanded. Once it had been through coercion, now it was through shame.

By now, Liam was five years old, and starting school. I went back to work; I did various jobs in catering and child-care. I was renting a new two-bedroom home, with a garden, around a 15-minute walk from my parents' house. I tried so hard to live in the moment, and not to look too far ahead.

But the spectre of the future court case lingered above me, sniggering at me and poking fun at my fear.

Around Christmas that same year, I started to feel very tired and under the weather.

"You look washed out, pet," Dad noticed. "Are you sleeping okay?"

I shrugged my shoulders.

"Same as usual, really," I said. "I never sleep that well."

Besides, Liam was a light sleeper and I was often up in the night with him. I was sleep-deprived like any mother of a young child.

But I felt ill too, all through the Christmas festivities, and my parents persuaded me to see the GP.

"Postnatal depression," he said immediately. "I think that's the problem."

He prescribed me some new medication, but that didn't work. I found myself back at the doctors' surgery, and this time, he suggested that maybe I was under stress.

"I've been under this stress for years," I told him. "I just don't believe that's my issue. It feels more of a physical thing."

For weeks, I was back and forth from the GP. I had several blood tests which all came back clear. By February, my skin was taking on a yellowish tinge, and I was becoming more and more concerned. I was exhausted too, barely able to drag myself through each day.

"I think this needs further investigation," the GP agreed.

I was admitted to hospital, and more tests showed that my liver function was very low. I was hooked up to a drip and prescribed a high dose of steroids.

"Your liver is not working very well," a consultant explained. "This could be the result of a viral infection. Maybe you've had a tattoo, or perhaps you picked it up in contaminated water."

I was perplexed. I hadn't had any tattoos. I didn't remember eating or drinking anything dodgy. But I couldn't help worrying about all the binge drinking and drug taking of my teenage years; I knew my liver was probably already overworked, without fighting a virus too.

"We'll do what we can," the consultant promised. "But your condition is very serious."

Over the next few days, I became seriously ill. I was rushed by ambulance from Huddersfield Royal Infirmary to the specialist liver unit at St James's University Hospital in Leeds. I drifted in and out of sleep and was aware, on the periphery of my consciousness, that Mum was at my bedside, holding my hand, every day. Most afternoons, Dad came with her for a short visit, bringing Liam with him too.

"Hang in there," he told me, with faint traces of his old soft Irish lilt.

But at one stage, I was given just 48 hours to live. My poor family were out of their minds with worry, but thankfully I was too heavily sedated to understand. And, as the hours crept agonisingly by, I began to improve. The steroids started to work, and I felt a little better, and a little more lucid.

Even so, I was in hospital for eight weeks, recovering day by day. Over the Easter weekend of 2017, I was well enough to sit up in bed and I flicked on the TV. The evening news came on, and I allowed myself a smile, wondering if

Dad was watching at home. The news had always been his favourite programme. Then, as I followed the next item, my blood ran cold.

"No!" I gasped, clapping my hand over my mouth.

Right there on the screen, in front of me, were members of the gang, being filmed as they walked into Kirklees Magistrates' Court. Alongside the footage was an account of the charges they were facing.

I was transfixed. It felt surreal, seeing the men, at once familiar yet strangely so removed, on a TV screen. Their actual faces were obscured, covered with blankets and coats. But I would have recognised them anywhere.

I'd had no idea they had been charged or that they were due before magistrates. I switched the TV off with trembling hands. It was really happening. We were really going to court.

* * * *

After I was discharged from hospital, I had to take a daily cocktail of medication, including steroids. The intravenous steroids had left me so puffy and bloated that I could barely move. I felt as though I had doubled in size. I moved back in with my parents temporarily, and lay on the sofa, hour after hour, weighed down with a mix of hopelessness and trepidation. Gradually, as my steroid dose was reduced, I began to feel better. But I was called in for six weekly hospital checks and was warned the condition would be with me for the rest of my life.

In May 2017, the ITV drama *Three Girls* was aired. It

told the story of child sexual exploitation and grooming in Rochdale, Greater Manchester, just a short journey from Huddersfield. I also heard about a *Panorama* programme on a grooming scandal in Rotherham, another working-class Northern town, which had been aired some months earlier.

"It might help you to watch those programmes," one of the police officers suggested. "Many of those girls have been through a similar ordeal to you."

But I shook my head. I couldn't begin to think about that. My own trauma was too much for me to cope with; I could not bear to hear about anyone else's.

In the months afterwards, Nazir Afzal, the former chief crown prosecutor for the North West, and Maggie Oliver, a former police detective, were often in the media speaking about the Rochdale scandal. But I couldn't bear to even read their interviews. It was all very well, people making films and giving opinions. But none of that helped me to piece my life back together. None of that helped me to get through each day. My behaviour was not so much selfish, but rather self-preservation. I knew I was close to cracking, and I had to do what I could to keep myself whole.

That autumn, we began planning in earnest for the forth-coming court case. I was introduced to the barrister for the prosecution, who showed me such kindness, but bowled me over with big words I had never heard of.

"You'll have to explain that again, please," I laughed, time after time.

At first, I opted to give evidence via video link, so that I would not have to go into the court building along with the defendants. But then, I changed my mind. I didn't want the gang to look at me, whilst I could not look at them. To me, that felt unfair.

"If they can see me, I feel as though they will still have control over me," I explained to the police.

I chose, instead, to give evidence, in the courtroom, from behind a blackout curtain.

In the weeks beforehand, I was taken on a visit to Leeds Crown Court to familiarise myself with the surroundings. A friendly police officer took Liam for a walk, up and down the corridors, whilst another officer showed me the modern and airy court room.

"I can do this," I told myself silently. "I can do it."

But I was not really convinced.

Then, days before the case was due to start, Dad called me to say his truck had been vandalised.

"Every single window smashed," he told me bitterly. "Glass all over the bloody path. It's a right mess."

We both knew exactly who was behind this.

"They know I need my truck for work," he continued. "This means I can't earn. And I'll have the expense of the repairs. Claiming on the insurance just isn't worth it, because my premium will go up."

My sympathy for Dad was drowned out by an immobilising terror. This was a warning from the gang. A clear sign that I should step away from the court case. What would they do next?

"I can't go to court," I babbled. "I just can't do it. They'll never leave us alone. This will never end."

Dad sighed. "I know you're scared, pet," he said gently. "But they are trying to intimidate us, that's all. They are bullies. There's no way I'm giving in. And neither should you.

"Go to court, tell the truth, with your head held high."

Tears pricked my eyes. It wasn't like Dad to make a big speech like that. And his words really touched my heart.

"You're right," I replied. "I can't pull out now. We need to tell the truth."

16

Trials and Tribulations

In November 2017, the court case began. Along with the other girls, I was being treated as a vulnerable witness, and the police had arranged to take me to and from the courts each day. That first morning, I was up and dressed way too early, pacing the kitchen, jittery and edgy from lack of sleep. I nibbled at the toast I'd made, but it went cold with a greasy film on top.

Mum was being called as a witness for the prosecution too and, for legal reasons, she and I were not allowed to discuss the case. We decided to limit all contact with each other so that we could not be accused of breaking the rules. Dad was looking after Liam, whilst we were both at court, and for the duration of the trial, I had agreed to stay at my own place alone. I would much rather have stayed with my parents and have them there to support me; even if it was just knowing that they were in the next room. I hated being on my own with my thoughts and fears and the constant self-reproach. But I understood it was vital not to prejudice the trial.

The police car arrived, with two officers in the front, and I sat in the back seat. At first, I tried to make light-hearted conversation, chatting about the snow that was forecast for the days ahead, and about my plans for the weekend.

"Bad traffic isn't it," I commented. "Rush hour, I suppose."

They chatted back, trying to fill the emptiness and keep me calm. But, as the journey progressed, I became transfixed by the numbers on the road signs. As they decreased, my stress levels increased: Leeds 10 miles, Leeds seven miles, Leeds three miles. It was a sinister countdown. Then, I spotted a cluster of high-rise flats which I knew, from my first visit, were not far from the court complex.

"You okay, Christina?" asked one of the officers. "You've gone very quiet."

I wanted to reply out of courtesy, but the words dried and shrivelled in my throat. My mind was wiped clean of thoughts. I was shaking so hard that as the car slowed and came to a stop, I could not even open the door to get out.

I was taken into the court building from the back entrance, and shown into a small witness room, below ground. There was a TV in there and a couple of chairs. Together with a police officer, I sat, awkwardly, with a polystyrene cup of weak tea cooling in my hands. I spent the time watching *Good Morning Britain* and *The Jeremy Kyle Show*, aware that I was making news whilst watching it also. Again, I tried to distract myself by concentrating on the TV or chatting to the female officer whose task it was to look after me. But it was both freaky and frightening knowing that my abusers were being sworn into the dock, right above me. Possibly the muffled noises I could hear were their own footsteps. Maybe they were just metres away from me. Closing my eyes, I could almost smell again the foul miasma of stale smoke, body odour and vodka.

When it was time for me to be taken up to the courtroom, I couldn't stop shivering, and yet I was sweating at the same time. I felt, inexplicably, as though I was the one on trial. I might as well have been walking towards the guillotine. I kept my eyes to the ground, as I walked into the courtroom. It was completely cleared, except for solicitors and barristers, so that I could be settled into place anonymously behind the curtain. It was a thick, dark curtain which drew right around the witness box, leaving me slightly in the dark, on every level. I felt as though I was in a very poky changing room. It was a cruel parallel; I couldn't remember the last time I'd been out shopping, trying on clothes, and buying myself something new. I couldn't remember the last time I'd felt like a typical young woman. My entire life seemed to revolve around the court case.

"Are you alright behind there?" my barrister asked.

I could hardly complain that I felt claustrophobic and trapped. That I was rattled by the realisation that my abusers would soon be led back into court, just a cotton curtain's width away from me. That I just wanted to be a normal girl, far away from here.

"Yes, I'm fine," I mumbled.

Cowering behind the curtain, I heard everyone else filing in; the jury, the public gallery, the press. And, of course, the defendants. I was completely hidden from view at all times, yet I felt so dreadfully naked and vulnerable. My face burned with shame and self-reproach. Even with a curtain around me, I felt a hundred pairs of eyes, boring through the barrier, scorching through to my blackened soul. Now, even now, with the men on trial and with me as a witness, I could not shake the sense that this was my fault. And I wondered whether I ever would.

Steeling myself, I pictured once again the ghostly little face of my lost daughter, Gracie; her life snuffed out, before it began, because of what I had endured at the hands of these men. They had forced me to get pregnant. And they had forced me to end that pregnancy too. A righteous anger bubbled within me. And from Gracie, and from her memory, I drew my strength.

"Yes, I am fine," I said again, louder, more self-assured.

The trial judge, Geoffrey Marson QC, had previously explained that Operation Tendersea, as the investigation was known, had been split into three trials, due to the sheer volume of defendants and victims. Tendersea, the court heard, concerned an investigation into the abduction, trafficking and sexual exploitation of young girls, myself included, in Huddersfield between 2004 and 2011. The trials would involve a staggering 28 defendants and over 150 counts, with the possibility of more to come.

I had previously been told I would be required to give evidence at all three trials and knew I had to brace myself for not one but three ordeals. For now, I could focus only on this first trial, which in itself was a huge overfacing.

Because there were multiple court cases, with some

defendants appearing in all trials, and some witnesses also, reporting restrictions were imposed to prevent prejudice. All reporting of the trial was banned throughout the media. I was in some ways relieved at the lack of media coverage. I understood I was entitled to automatic anonymity, as an alleged victim of a sexual attack. But to me, that made little difference. The anonymity only went so far. I knew who I was, after all. I knew this was about me and I could never forget that. I could not escape myself. And there was an illogical feeling also that the anonymity somehow confirmed that I had something to hide, and that I therefore carried some shame and responsibility.

Giving evidence behind a curtain had that same double-edged effect; whilst I was relieved and thankful not to have to face my abusers, I also felt I was being hidden away and my role as victim and witness was something to be ashamed of.

But overall, I was glad the case was not being reported, day to day. I wasn't sure I could have coped with seeing the defendants' names and faces plastered on the front of every newspaper, and on every social media platform. The trial would have been the main topic of discussion and gossip in every shop and on every bus and in every queue, in Huddersfield and beyond. With the reporting restrictions, I would at least be spared that.

Prosecutor Richard Wright QC told the court: "These men cared only for themselves and viewed the girls as objects to be used and abused at will…

"The defendants used alcohol, drugs and violence to bend the girls to their will."

The court heard many of the girls targeted were socially isolated and as such became "easy targets for abuse". Among the victims were girls with mild learning disabilities, girls who were bullied at school, and one girl whose mother was completely unable to look after her because of her own drink and drug problems.

As a result the court was told that the girls often craved the attention they were given, leaving them at a loss to see what was being done to them until it was too late. Some of the victims had even believed they were in genuine relationships; such was the depth to which they had been groomed.

When I was called upon to give my evidence, I told the court: "I suppose when you're young and you get bullied at school you do sort of like the attention, and things getting bought for you and stuff, but then once you were in with them you couldn't get out of it…

"They got your trust and then stuff would start happening to you and it's just one of those things that you couldn't get out of, it just happened… My mum and dad's house got trashed, their cars got trashed… I was constantly getting raped and beaten up."

I was frightened, speaking out, in front of the court. My voice, slightly muffled by the curtain, wavered and shook.

"Speak up, please," said the judge,

"Sorry," I said, clearing my throat.

I tried again. But I was so nervous, I could barely make myself heard. It was hot and stuffy too, behind the curtain, and I felt tiny droplets of sweat running down my spine. Could I do this? I summoned every last shred of courage that I had.

Yet alongside my terror, I felt too, a dawning relief, and even a faint glow of pride, that I had finally done it. The truth was out there. I had done my bit.

The court was again cleared whilst I was taken back to the witness room, and, in my place, another girl spoke of truanting from school in order to meet the men.

She said: "They would start giving us alcohol and offering us cannabis to smoke and we thought 'yes, we like this, we're going to do this, we're grown up'.

"But we weren't really, we were young, but when you are young you do think it is cool to be doing them things, going against what your mum says and stuff like that.

"Just having a little drink, having a bit of a laugh and then as the weeks went on, it started getting a bit different; the drinks would taste a bit different than what they did and you can't really remember things."

Other girls spoke of being scared by threats and violence to them and their families. One girl said: "There were so many of them, they all knew each other, and it was like an escalation and they knew they could pick me up whenever they wanted because my mum was vulnerable."

Another victim said: "It was just like a continual lifestyle. I didn't know how to get out of it.

"You feel manipulated and scared in a way that if you don't meet these guys then something is going to happen and it just went on continuously for like years really, just the same thing – day in, day out.

"You would see people with knives or fighting so you do feel scared, and you do feel intimidated.

"But on the other side you feel like you want to be a rebel because you're that age. But really it's a downright dangerous situation you are in and you are playing with fire... getting driven to Scammonden Dam at 13 years old at two o'clock in the morning and if you don't do this you're not gonna come back.

"I always bugged myself – 'why did I go back?' – and I still cannot answer that question. For years and years I blamed myself that it was my fault I went back.

"They're quite manipulative and when you're in that situation you're so pressured, you feel stupid and dirty and horrible."

Another witness, explaining the reasons why she kept going back to the gang said: "They just threatened me – 'I'm coming to pick you up now and if you don't come, I'm coming to get your mum'."

The court was told that parents had to call police because their children became so aggressive when they tried to prevent them from leaving the family home. One parent received a threatening phone call asking for their daughter and was told: "I'm coming for you."

That same mother received a phone call from one of the other girls asking her to pick her daughter up. She was found on Crosland Moor, Huddersfield, propped up against a wall, unable to stand and disorientated.

Families became very afraid, the court heard, because the men knew where they all lived. They complained of being followed home and receiving constant abusive phone calls to their homes and mobiles. At least one girl attempted suicide.

One of the girls was seen being thrown out of a moving car outside her home. She had cuts and bruises on her face and was under the influence of alcohol. The brother of one of the girls saw a car with Asian men inside and they said that they were looking for "white girls or bitches".

House windows were smashed, threats were made to cause physical harm to members of the girls' families. Threats were also made, the court was told, to bomb a house and damage was done to cars, including loosening wheel nuts, which caused the potential for serious danger.

When one girl was taken into care she was later abducted from the foster home and supplied with drugs and sexually abused. Such was the extent of the men's hold over the girls that one woman described how her daughter cracked her head jumping from a first floor balcony at their home in order to get out to see them.

The girl later told police: "Every time I went out something bad happened. I risked my life every time. I was a mess."

One victim, who only escaped her abusers when her family was forced to move out of the area following a house fire, said: "It was the best thing I ever did, and that's bad saying that burning your house down is the best thing you ever did."

The evidence of each girl, myself included, ran along eerily similar lines. There were 15 of us called as witnesses in total. 15 broken lives. 15 shattered families. It should have been some comfort to learn that the other girls felt afraid and trapped. That they too feared for their lives and their families' lives. That they too blamed themselves, just as I did. We should have felt a sense of sisterhood, the solace of a shared burden, an understanding that we at least were not suffering alone. But it was too late for that. We had been turned and pitted against each other too many times. Pretos had set us up as enemies, as snitches, as rivals to each other. As much as I might have longed to reach out to the other girls after the case was finished and I was legally allowed, I knew I never would or could. They were my former friends and my fellow victims. We had shared unimaginable trauma, lodged deep within us all. Yet they were strangers to me now.

* * * *

One morning, when the police came to pick me up for court, the long-awaited snow was starting to fall heavily. Our journey to Leeds was slow and stop-start, with traffic building up as the flakes settled, and I could see we were facing long delays.

"We're not going to make it on time, today," the driver told me. "This snow is coming down fast."

As we crawled laboriously along the motorway, I followed the countdown on the road signs, unable even to enjoy the magic of the snow because of what lay ahead. It wasn't long before I spotted the high-rise buildings in the distance, and my heart jumped and stuttered. As much as I wanted to fast-forward into the future and for the trial to be over, I wanted to push it right back into the past, too. I would have liked to spend the entire day in the snowy traffic jam and to never reach the high-rises. But inexorably and unforgivingly, the journey continued, and we eventually arrived at court.

"Don't worry about the delay," a court official told us. "I think everyone has been hit by the snow."

It turned out that Mum had been held up by the weather too, she was late to court because her car had broken down the day before and she was using public transport. When she got onto the stand, she was frazzled and apprehensive.

"Have you had any contact with your daughter?" demanded the defence barrister.

"Not this morning," Mum replied. "I came straight to court."

"And yesterday?" he asked.

"Actually no, my car broke down and my husband had to come and collect the vehicle and arrange a recovery."

The defence barrister seized on this fact immediately, quizzing her about the details of the breakdown.

"And your husband can vouch that you didn't discuss the case, with him or with your daughter?" he insisted.

"Yes of course," she said. "I asked him to collect my car. That's all."

But the defence insisted on bringing Dad to court for his version of events. He hated formal occasions and was flustered and overwhelmed to find himself called urgently to the witness box, that same afternoon, still wearing his work clothes and his builder's boots. He had not been listed as a witness previously and he looked absolutely bewildered as he stared around the court and confirmed exactly what Mum had said.

"She doesn't discuss the case with me or with our daughter or with anyone at all," he told them.

He was then allowed to leave and go back to work. I felt a hissing fury rising up my throat when I heard about the wholly pointless fiasco later. The gang was controlling me and my family – even now – in a court of law. My parents were being made to jump through legal hoops to prove they were honest and trustworthy. Ironically, they were the only people in this entire unholy mess who had behaved with decency and honour.

"They are not the ones on trial here," I complained. "This is not fair. My dad should not have been dragged to court like that."

But there was nothing we could do about it. That night, on my journey home in the police car, again through thick sludge and snow, my phone rang. When my mother's name flashed up on the screen, I gulped.

"It's my mum," I told the officers. "I can't answer it. I can't have any contact with her just in case I'm accused of breaking the rules. But she wouldn't ring unless it was important. There might be a problem at home. What shall I do?"

"Why not answer it on loudspeaker?" suggested one of the officers. "That way, we can listen in to your conversation and monitor the content."

As I answered, I heard Liam's excited voice. He had borrowed Mum's phone to call me because his news simply could not wait.

"Mummy!" he announced. "Guess what? I built a snowman outside with Grandad!"

All tensions diffused, I smiled.

"That's lovely darling," I replied. "I can't wait to see you soon. But I have to go now."

The officers laughed too as I hung up.

But it bothered me that something as simple and innocent as my own son building a snowman had the potential to create so much drama. On top of all the stress of the court case, and the memories it evoked, avoiding members of my own family was very hard. I understood why. But again, it felt like I was being penalised. It felt like I was the one on trial.

* * * *

As the days passed, that feeling only intensified and at times, it threatened to engulf me completely. In court, I was questioned for hours at a time, day after day after day.

The defence barristers – one for each defendant – picked at me and grilled me each in turn until I felt like a dishcloth, wrung out to dry. Like all the last drops of life and vitality had been squeezed right out of me.

It was the same tack from each barrister too. They suggested I had wanted relationships with the men and I had gone back to them, time after time. Which was, of course, partly true. They also claimed the men had taken an interest in my life and my career.

"You wanted to be a beautician," said one of the barristers. "You confided in my client."

"Not exactly," I replied shortly. "I wanted to be a hairdresser."

It was a minor detail. But even so, if I had shared my career plans with my abusers, I didn't see what difference that made. Yes, I had wanted to go back to them, yes I had told them about myself. Yes, they knew I was a child. Yes, they had groomed and brainwashed me, abused and raped me. Surely this line of questioning was further proof – not justification – of the gang's guilt?

There was no defence for targeting young girls, plying them with drink and drugs, and forcing them to have sex. None at all. I wanted to scream it out loud at the barristers, I wanted to stand on my chair, rip back the curtain, and make the announcement to the world. But instead I hung my head in shame and mumbled my replies.

Giving evidence, day after day, was traumatising. The witness box felt like a platform for the gang to get at me and the curtain was only a partial shield. For though my face was obscured, my voice was not. And listening to their barristers, it felt as though none of them believed me. They pulled me apart, emotionally and mentally, until I felt small, insignificant and worthless. Grubby and tainted, and no more valuable than a stain on the sole of a shoe. Each night, after giving evidence, I took long showers, washing my hair, scrubbing at my scalp and my skin. I used up all the hot water, standing under the stream until it grew cool. But I just could not get clean. I just could not *feel* clean.

My moods, on those evenings, were very low. Often, in the house on my own, I cried right through the early hours, until I found respite, albeit temporary, in sleep. And even then, the gang members invaded my dreams. I had recurring nightmares about being trapped in Pretos' car, where we were submerged in a lake of some sort. Perhaps it was the reservoir, perhaps it was the sailing club lake. I never found out. With water rising at the windows, I would plead hysterically with the men to let me out. It was a vicious circle; I knew that by crying and showing weakness, they would punish me all the more. Yet as the water level grew higher and higher, I could not help but scream and beg for my life.

"Please!" I yelled. "Let me out! I'm drowning!"

Pretos turned towards me from the driver's seat, but in place of his face was an empty hole. There were no eyes, no nose, no mouth. And yet his neck and body were just as I remembered, right down to his grey tracksuit.

He did not speak, but instead stretched out his hand, unfurling his fingers which were full of ecstasy pills. Grabbing my head with his other hand, he forced my hair back and rammed my mouth full of pills. In that moment, the dirty water from the lake began rushing in through the cracks in the windows and doors. I was choking on a mix of dirty water and drugs. My mouth was packed full, and I could not scream, and anyway, there was nobody there to hear me. This was the end of me.

When I awoke, I was still coughing and spluttering, trying to clear my airways. I took deep breaths. But there was little comfort in being awake. I wasn't trapped in the car, and I wasn't being force-fed drugs by Pretos. But I was still drowning. And I was still choking. A little bit more, each day, in court.

The trial moved on smoothly, in contrast to the turmoil I

felt inside. The court was told that victims and their families, mine included, claimed to have repeatedly told police and the authorities what was happening at the time, but no action was taken.

One woman said she had even written to the Prime Minister. Others had contacted their MP and support groups. Some had sought legal advice.

One girl said when she tried to tell two officers who took her to hospital after she was assaulted by one of her abusers, they told her: "You must have wanted it."

The court was told that the first allegations to be taken seriously surfaced in 2011 when a victim wrote a letter to a judge outlining the abuse she had suffered, but she did not make a formal complaint. It was not until 2013 that another complaint was made and an investigation was launched. Over the following three years, dozens of girls and men were interviewed.

I thought back to my 2011 interview in prison – and how my statement had slipped unnoticed down the back of a dusty filing cabinet – and I felt a surge of resentment and irritation.

Why hadn't they listened to me then? Maybe other girls might have been saved from that point onwards. If only someone had taken me seriously. I remembered the prison chaplain, the first person, the only person, to really hear my voice. I hoped that one day, when the trial was over, she would realise that she had played a pivotal part.

Amere Singh Dhaliwal, 35, also known as Pretos, was described in court as the ringleader of the gang. The court was told he was married with children of his own.

I was repulsed. To think of him with a family and with young children was sickening. I imagined him collecting his children from school, making breakfast in bed for his wife, attending parents' evenings and school fairs. The paradox was grotesque.

Dhaliwal was charged with 54 separate offences, including 22 rapes, involving 11 girls, of which I was one. Many of the other gang members faced similar charges. Some had fled the country overseas. Some were lying low elsewhere. Some, I simply had never been able to identify.

14 weeks and two days later, the first trial finally drew to a close. I was absolutely exhausted, mentally and physically, and so confused that I had no idea whether or not the men would be convicted. A small part of me was even worried that the trial judge might blame all of this on me.

The jury of six men and five women took 30 hours to deliver their verdicts.

I stayed at home for the closing speeches of the trial and later the verdicts; I didn't want to be in court for a moment longer than was necessary. Yet I found myself hovering by my phone, uptight and restless. When it rang, I snatched it up, knowing it was one of the officers I'd been working with.

"Guilty, guilty, guilty, guilty," she said. "It goes on and on. Well done Christina. You did it."

"I did," I replied slowly.

Two men were acquitted. But eight men, including Pretos, were convicted of 85 offences.

At the end of that first trial, the judge said: "The way you treated these girls defies understanding; this abuse was vile and wicked. As cases of sexual abuse with which the courts have to deal, this case comes at the top of the scale. None of you has expressed any remorse for what you did."

Their lack of regret did not surprise me in any way. Never once had they shown remorse or even a sliver of empathy for me or the other girls.

I had expected, hoped maybe, for a sense of achievement and celebration at the verdicts. But this was no time to gloat. I found I could barely smile as I ended the call. The men were guilty. But of course, I had known that all along.

****

The second trial began in April 2018.

I had hoped this one might be in some way easier because I had been through it all before. But if anything, now that I knew what was ahead, it felt so much worse. I dreaded the cross-examination, from one defence barrister after another, prodding at me and pulling me apart, like meat off a bone. I just didn't feel there was any of me left.

Though there had been no reporting of the first trial in the media, there was a lot of public interest. Operation Tendersea had attracted wide-spread fury and disgust from all sections of society, and feelings were running high. I was warned to prepare myself for chaos at the court.

As before, it was arranged that two police officers would collect me and bring me home each day. Mum was required as a witness in this trial also and we were not allowed to discuss the trial and limited all communication with her.

Once again, I was juggling a stack of practical obstacles with the weight of the emotional strain.

The first morning that I was due to give my evidence, we went into the court, through the back entrance, as planned, and I was taken to a small room with a police officer. I waited for a while, and nothing happened. There were no updates from the case, and neither was I called to appear. The hours dragged by, and I became increasingly fidgety.

"Can I go out for a bit of fresh air?" I asked an officer. "I really need to stretch my legs. I'd like a cigarette too."

But she shook her head.

"Sorry, you have to stay in here for your own safety," she replied.

I was mystified, and more than a little afraid too. The entire morning passed and, as lunchtime came, I grew more and more impatient.

"I can't stay in here all day," I protested. "What's going on? Why won't you tell me? This is a complete waste of all of our time."

As the courts closed, I was again collected by the two police officers, and driven back home. Nobody could tell me what on earth was going on.

It was only that night that I heard a huge EDL demonstration outside the court had caused mayhem. Tommy Robinson, the EDL founder, had broadcast a Facebook Live outside Leeds Crown Court.

Because there were reporting restrictions, there was now a very real chance that the trial could collapse, costing tens of thousands of pounds, and more importantly, potentially costing us the chance of justice. Several of the defence barristers, I learned, had already swooped on this unexpected gift for their clients and had applied to have the jury discharged.

I was furious. Tommy Robinson had never met us. He had no idea of what we had been through. I felt strongly that he was hijacking our trauma, jumping aboard our misery, just to make a name for himself. The reporting restrictions had nothing to do with race or religion. They were simply in place to ensure a fair trial. This was not about skin colour or culture. This was about right and wrong. This was about justice.

I knew that my parents would be livid too. They, like me, were under so much stress. They had given so much of themselves to the judicial process, as I had. Yet of course I wasn't allowed to ask them about it because we, unlike some, were sticking to the rules and not discussing the trial at all.

Tommy Robinson's broadcast, and the chaos which followed, was further salt in our already smarting wounds. It was more pressure and more stress, and I felt I could not cope with it.

In the end, after legal argument, the second trial went ahead, and I faced a string of cross-examinations from a new set of barristers in front of a new jury. As I gave my final piece of evidence, I felt absolutely exhausted.

And completely worthless.

The barristers seemed to have the knack of dismantling me as a person and handing me back all the pieces, higgledy-piggledy, after their questions were finished. Try as I might,

I could not put myself back together as I had once been; like an imperfect jigsaw, there was always something missing.

The second trial lasted six weeks and five days and concluded in June 2018. A jury of six women and six men took 23 hours 43 minutes to deliver their verdicts.

Again, my celebrations were muted. I remained at home and waited for a call from the police to confirm the verdicts.

"All guilty!" the officer announced.

Eight men were convicted of 26 offences and none of the defendants were acquitted. Again, I felt that I should be whooping and punching the air in victory. But any show of celebration would be contrived and false. I felt strangely flat. It was like I'd been walking around for 13 years with a broken neck with everyone telling me I was a hypochondriac. Now finally, an X-ray had shown I had been telling the truth all along. I felt relief, but I also felt great sadness. People were only telling me what I'd known all along. And I feared too that a broken neck might be easier to fix than the damage I had suffered.

The third trial began in September that same year and concluded in October. This one lasted three weeks but by now, I was losing all sense of time and structure. I seemed to exist only to be transported to and from court and to stand behind a curtain listening to strangers making horrific allegations about me. In-between the trial dates, I had hospital appointments and check-ups, monitoring the progress of my recovery from liver damage.

For almost two days, I was cross-examined by a string of different barristers, each representing one of the gang members. Three victims, myself included, who had all given evidence in at least one of the previous trials, gave evidence again.

On this occasion, a jury of eight women and four men took five hours and one minute to deliver verdicts. Four men were convicted of 10 offences. None of the defendants were acquitted.

And, for a third time, the sense of relief outweighed any feelings of victory.

* * * *

It was reported that Tommy Robinson had been jailed for breaching the reporting restrictions during the second trial. The matter was not reported during the trials but a court was told that the founder of the English Defence League was jailed over comments which had the potential to cause a retrial at Leeds Crown Court.

The court heard that Robinson, whose real name is Stephen Christopher Yaxley-Lennon, streamed an hour-long Facebook Live broadcast outside the court and within hours it had been watched more than 250,000 times.

Judge Geoffrey Marson QC, who jailed the far-right activist for 13 months for contempt of court, told him his actions could have caused the long-running Operation Tendersea trial to be retried, which would cost taxpayers "hundreds and hundreds of thousands of pounds".

A court order had been in place temporarily banning any reporting on Robinson's arrest and sentencing hearing.

The 35-year-old was arrested on suspicion of a breach of the peace on the day of the broadcast and was held in the court cells before being taken up to the courtroom to face the trial judge. In an unusual move, he had been arrested, charged and sentenced within five hours.

The video footage was played to the judge as Robinson sat in the dock. He had a previous conviction for contempt of court, receiving a suspended prison sentence after he had been filming inside Canterbury Crown Court. He pleaded guilty to contempt of court and breach of a suspended sentence.

Matthew Harding, mitigating, said his client felt "deep regret" after realising the potential consequences of his actions.

He said Robinson was aware of the reporting restriction in place in the case but thought what he was saying on camera was in fact already in the public domain.

The barrister added: "He was mindful, having spoken to others and taken advice, not to say things that he thought would actually prejudice these proceedings.

"He did not try to cause difficulties for the court process."

Mr Harding said Robinson had been the victim of assaults while serving time in prison in the past and claimed there had been "a price on his head" during his last prison term, with inmates being offered the reward of drugs and mobile phones to kill him.

But the judge said: "No one could possibly conclude that it would be anything other than highly prejudicial to the defendants in the trial.

"I respect everyone's right to free speech. That's one of the most important rights that we have.

"With those rights come responsibilities. The responsibility to exercise that freedom of speech within the law. I am not sure you appreciate the potential consequence of what you have done."

Robinson had served two months in jail before being freed after the finding of contempt was overturned by the Court of Appeal in August 2018.

But the case was then referred back to the Attorney General, who announced that it was in the public interest to bring fresh proceedings against Robinson, and he was found to be in contempt of court by High Court judges. He was jailed and served nine weeks in prison before being released.

17

Judgement Day

In October 2018, the police arranged for us to go to Bradford Crown Court to watch the sentencing live, via video link, from all three trials. Dad, uncharacteristically confrontational, insisted he would rather go to the sentencing in person at Leeds Crown Court.

"I want to look those animals in the eye," he said. "I want to be there."

But the police explained they were expecting demonstrations and possible unrest outside the court, and the presence of the victims might only inflame the situation and cause us more stress. And for my part, I felt much more comfortable linking up via a screen. I did not want to face the men again.

On the morning of the sentencing, we gathered in the courtroom, and the tension was palpable, not just with the prospect of the sentencing, but also between ourselves. The other girls were there, in the same room, and a braver part of me wanted to run over and put my arms around them. But instead, I stood and smiled awkwardly. Our communication went no further than that. There was no olive branch, no slender strand of hope. They were the only ones who knew exactly how I felt, who had walked in my shoes. But the tragic consequences of our shared trauma were that we were doomed to suffer alone.

Now, even now, as I took my seat in the court, I could not believe that the men were going to face punishment. All those years of suffering and control. It all came down to this. As the judge cleared his throat and began to speak, a hush fell over the room, as though a large blanket had been thrown over us all. I was glued to the video-link, my insides churning, one hand nervously tapping against the other.

"You're doing fine, pet," Dad whispered.

And so, it began:

Amere Singh Dhaliwal, or 'Pretos', of Huddersfield and aged 35, was convicted of 54 offences. They were 22 counts of rape, 13 counts of trafficking for sexual exploitation, five counts of inciting a child to engage in sexual activity, three counts of sexual assault, three counts of supplying a controlled drug of Class A, three counts of possessing an indecent image of a child, two counts of administering a substance with intent, one count of inciting child prostitution, one count of assault by penetration and one count of racially aggravated assault. He was jailed for life with a minimum of 17 years and 312 days.

Dad-of-four Irfan Ahmed, aged 34, of Huddersfield, and known as 'Finny', was a former cannabis dealer and was convicted of two counts of trafficking for sexual exploitation and one count of sexual activity with a child. He was jailed for eight years.

Zahid Hassan, 29, also of Huddersfield and nicknamed

'Little Manny,' was a takeaway worker who had groomed a vulnerable child, aged 11 or 12, using food. He was convicted of 14 offences. They were six counts of rape, two counts of abduction of a child, two counts of supplying a controlled drug of Class A, one count of sexual assault, one count of trafficking for sexual exploitation, one count of attempted rape and one count of racially aggravated assault. He was jailed for 18 years.

Mohammed Kammer, 34, of Paddock, Huddersfield, who went by the name 'Kammy', was convicted of two counts of rape. He was jailed for 16 years and would be eligible to apply for release on licence in June 2026.

Mohammed Rizwan Aslam, or 'Big Riz,' aged 31, of Dewsbury, West Yorks, was convicted of two counts of rape. He was jailed for 15 years, eligible to apply for release on licence on December 7, 2025. Aslam's previous convictions included assault occasioning actual bodily harm and being concerned in the supply of heroin.

Abdul Rehman, 31, of Sheffield, known as 'Beastie', was an aspiring pharmacist and cannabis dealer. He was convicted of rape, trafficking for sexual exploitation, supplying a controlled drug of Class C and assault occasioning actual bodily harm. He was jailed for 16 years.

Raj Singh Barsran, 34, of Huddersfield, whose nickname was 'Raj', had hosted many of the parties where girls were sexually abused. Previous convictions included handling stolen goods, possession with intent to supply cannabis and wounding with intent. He was convicted of two counts of sexual assault and one count of rape. He was jailed for 17 years, eligible to apply for release on licence on December 7, 2026.

Taxi driver Nahman Mohammed, known as 'Dracula' or 'Drac', 33, of Paddock, Huddersfield, had previously been convicted of driving over the prescribed limit and harassment. He was convicted of two counts of rape and one count of trafficking for sexual exploitation. He was jailed for 15 years and could apply for release on licence in December 2025.

Mansoor Akhtar, 27, of Huddersfield, nicknamed 'Boy', was already serving a six-year prison sentence for his part in a different grooming gang. He was convicted of two counts of rape and two counts of trafficking for sexual exploitation. He was jailed for eight years and was potentially eligible for release on licence in 2023.

Wiqas Mahmud, 38, of Golcar, known as 'Vic', was convicted of three counts of rape. He was jailed for 15 years and would be eligible to apply for release on licence on December 22, 2025.

Married father Nasarat Hussain, known as 'Nurse', aged 30, and from Huddersfield, was convicted of three counts of rape and one count of sexual assault. He was jailed for 17 years. His previous convictions included assault and possession with intent to supply Class A drugs.

Sajid Hussain, 33, of Huddersfield, nicknamed 'Fish', was convicted of two counts of rape. He went on the run after the jury went out to deliberate and was sentenced in his absence to 17 years' imprisonment.

Mohammed Irfraz, or 'Faj', aged 30, from Huddersfield,

was convicted of one count of abduction of a child and two counts of trafficking for sexual exploitation. He was jailed for six years, eligible to apply for release on licence in 2021. His previous convictions included common assault and motoring offences.

Married father-of-three Faisal Nadeem, or 'Chiller', aged 32, was convicted of rape and supplying a controlled drug of Class A. He was jailed for 12 years. He later appealed against the sentence, arguing that Robinson's live video had prejudiced the trial, but his permission to appeal was refused by a Court of Appeal judge. His previous convictions included threatening behaviour, common assault, robbery, witness intimidation and possession of Class A and B drugs. Along with Zubair Ahmed, he had also been charged with possession of extreme pornography, specifically an image of sexual intercourse with a horse. But there was no evidence produced against them and the charge was dropped.

Mohammed Azeem, or 'Mosabella', 33, of Bradford, was convicted of five counts of rape. His previous convictions included assault, theft and breach of court orders. He was jailed for 18 years.

Drug addict and dealer Manzoor Hassan, 38, of Lockwood, and known also as 'Big Manny,' was already serving a seven-and-a-half-year prison sentence for making a schoolgirl work as a prostitute. He was convicted of administering a noxious substance, inciting a person aged under 18 to become a prostitute and supplying a controlled drug of Class A. He was jailed for five years, eligible to apply for release in 2023. He already had a previous conviction for supplying heroin.

Married Mohammed Akram, 33, of Huddersfield and nicknamed 'Kid', was convicted of two counts of trafficking for sexual exploitation and two counts of rape. He was jailed for 17 years.

Niaz Ahmed, 54 of Huddersfield, known as 'Shaq', was convicted of inciting a child to engage in sexual activity and sexual assault. He was handed a five-year sentence.

Mohammed Imran Ibrar, known as 'Bully' and aged 34 and of Huddersfield, was convicted of trafficking for sexual exploitation and assault occasioning actual bodily harm. He was sentenced to three years eligible for release on licence in 2021.

Asif Bashir, 33, of, Huddersfield, nicknamed 'Junior,' was convicted of rape and attempted rape. He was jailed for 11 years.

The group of 20 men were convicted of offences against 15 young girls and received jail sentences totalling 257 years. It was the biggest scandal ever to hit Huddersfield and the gang was the largest to be convicted of sex abuse in the UK.

Of that total, 11 men were convicted of offences against me including 22 counts of rape, inciting sexual activity, indecent images of a child, trafficking, attempted rape, racially aggravated assault, supply of Class A drugs, sexual assault and inciting sexual activity.

Hearing it all read out in court was mind-blowing. Part of me was amazed I had survived it; stunned that I had not crumbled under such unrelenting evil. But at the same time, these men were so familiar to me and the crimes they had been jailed for formed a regular part of my daily life. It was an odd and unsettling paradox and one which I knew I would never reconcile in my mind.

Describing the abuse, Judge Marson said: "The details were chilling. It was persistent and prolonged.

"Having been plied with alcohol and drugs, girls were raped, they were trafficked to isolated areas or to houses for the purpose of sexual abuse by those who took them or by others.

"When taken to isolated places such as the moors or a reservoir, if they didn't comply, they were, on occasions, beaten.

"They were told they would be left to make their own way back, children on their own, children late at night in isolated areas.

"They were taken to so-called parties at houses where there would be older Asian men.

"Again they were plied with alcohol and drugs, on occasion drinks were spiked and many times these girls were rendered senseless.

"They would be taken to a room where, one by one, men would go and abuse these girls sexually.

"Sometimes no contraception was used, sometimes plastic bags were used as condoms.

"It was disgusting and degrading."

The judge continued: "They were raped and sexually abused in cars, car parks, houses, a snooker centre, a takeaway, in a park and other places.

"It is clear that once the will of these girls had been overborne, they continued to be plied with alcohol and drugs and they were controlled by violence and/or the threat of violence, either to them personally or to their families."

Judge Marson continued: "Some were almost senseless when they arrived home.

"Many came home injured, having been sexually assaulted.

"(Two victims) were forced to commit crime and served substantial custodial sentences for it.

"Girls repeatedly went back knowing they would be abused, because they were too frightened for themselves and their families not to. These girls changed beyond recognition."

The judge added: "They thought that these men were showing them genuine affection, but what in fact was happening was that a relationship of trust was created, albeit that it was entirely false and had been deliberately created to enable predatory men such as you to perpetrate gross sexual abuse for your own perverted gratification.

"For some it was a more exciting way of life, they saw it as being more adult, doing things which other girls of their age were not doing."

In conclusion, he said: "The sentences I pass on you are severe and are intended to be so. They are intended to deter others from behaving in this way."

And to Pretos, he said: "Your treatment of these girls was inhuman… You treated them as commodities to be passed around for your own sexual gratification and the gratification of others. The extent and gravity of your offending far exceeds anything which I have previously encountered. It was a very significant campaign of rape and other sexual abuse.

"Children's lives have been ruined and families profoundly affected by seeing their children, over months and years, out of control, having been groomed by you and other members of your gang."

* * * *

After the sentencing was over, Dad and I walked out into the autumn sunshine, and I blinked in surprise at the daylight. Everything seemed brighter and more brittle. I had hoped, after listening to the sentences, to feel a sense of calm and closure. Instead, I experienced a rush of adrenalin and agitation. I felt panicked, though I didn't understand why. I tried to focus on the memory of my unborn baby, my little Gracie. I hoped she was proud, I hoped she knew I had done this for her, for Liam, for the safety of all children.

"Let's go for a full Wetherspoon's," Dad suggested, sensing how uneasy I was. "I think we deserve it."

Breathing slowly, I tried to calm myself down as we waited for our order.

"It's over," I told myself. "It's all over."

And as we tucked into our bacon and eggs, Dad paused and smiled.

"Well, you did it, pet," he said. "I'm so proud of you. I can't tell you how much. These monsters are all going to prison. They're off the streets. The girls in Huddersfield are safe. And that's partly thanks to you. You made the first statement, and you were there at the forefront of the police investigation. You're stronger than anyone I know."

I blinked back the tears. Dad wasn't given to over-emotional speeches and his words really pulled at my heartstrings. And in that moment, as I speared a slice of bacon with my fork, it really did seem that straightforward. The baddies were in prison. The goodies had got justice. We could all move on and forget about the past.

If only life was that simple.

****

In the days after the sentencing was made public, the case was reported right across the UK media and beyond. It was impossible to scroll through social media or to flick on the TV without hearing about the infamous Huddersfield Grooming Gang. The sheer size of the trial – the biggest ever grooming scandal in the UK – and also public outrage that the victims had been ignored for so long – meant that it was of interest to all levels of the media.

In vain, I tried to slot back into normal life, whatever that was, and pretend somehow that I was not one of the girls that the whole country seemed to be talking about. In the media, I was referred to as Girl A, and my evidence from court was now being reported by several publications. I just wanted to forget it, to slough off my old life like a surplus skin. But it was all everyone could think of. And it was all I could think of, too. I felt as though was in limbo, suspended in some sort of no-man's land, whilst a media feeding frenzy went on around me:

Some newspapers ran lurid and grotesque headlines:

'Vile and wicked Asian grooming gang jailed…..
'Girl forced to have sex with 300 men by the age of 15.'
'Twisted nicknames…revealed in gruesome court trials.'

Other publications spoke of "a polarised debate between those who argue that these men's race and faith are the main factors driving these crimes on the one hand and those who strenuously deny that they play a role at all".

Everyone seemed to have an opinion and a worthy point of view.

One article continued: "Asian men are more likely to work in the night-time economy, which gives them greater opportunity to exploit vulnerable children."

That observation was so ridiculous, it made me want to laugh out loud. I really didn't think that shift work was the root of the problem. There were plenty of decent adults living perfectly blameless lives whilst working in the 'night-time economy'.

And it went on:

"It would be preposterous to suggest that the sexual exploitation of children is concentrated among people of a particular ethnicity: it goes on everywhere. But it is certainly plausible that within different cultures sexual abuse might take different forms, or manifest itself in different ways, and, if so, it is crucial to understand that."

These journalists and academics might as well have been on a different planet to me. Ethnicity must, logically, have played a role in the grooming since all of my abusers were of Asian heritage. But that does not mean it was a race issue. Cultural, perhaps, to a certain extent. But clearly there are white paedophile gangs too. For me, the skin colour of the abusers was not important. The problem with these monsters was on the inside, not the outside. The more I read in the media, the more depressed I felt. So much was mis-infor-mation. At best, I felt judged and patronised by high-brow writers who knew nothing of what I had been through, less still how to fix it. At worst, I felt raw and exposed and com-pletely valueless. And still – and it made me want to scream out loud – still, I felt guilty. So guilty. I just could not help it.

On one level, I was pleased by the sentencing. I felt I had done something good for the next generation and for myself. I had spoken out, and people had listened. My voice was heard, and I was grateful for that. But the fear and shame remained. I felt vindicated and I felt listened to. But I also felt drained and damaged.

And, after the initial agitated euphoria had subsided, I was left empty and scooped out. There was a lingering sense of regret, a stain I could not scrub away, no matter how hard I tried. I had expected to feel happy and victorious. I had been looking forward to closure. I had been looking forward to moving on with my life. Yet it was not so easy.

And the reminders continued. It seemed that every agency wanted to have their say.

Detective Chief Inspector Ian Mottershaw, from West Yorkshire Police, who led the investigation, said: "First and most importantly, I would like to pay tribute to each and every victim who came forward firstly to report these heinous crimes, but to go through the gruelling court process which has taken nearly a year to conclude and to bravely give their accounts to us and the court. I cannot praise them enough for their courage and tenacity in helping us secure justice for them against these defendants.

"The investigation into this case has been extremely complex and the investigative team have worked tirelessly for the past five years to ensure that no stone has been left unturned. We welcome the convictions and sentences which have been passed down throughout the year to these depraved individuals, who subjected vulnerable young children to unthinkable sexual and physical abuse.

"Child sexual exploitation is abhorrent and is one of the most important challenges facing the police. Safeguarding the vulnerable and protecting victims is West Yorkshire Police's top priority. It is totally unacceptable and it is the responsibility of all agencies, communities and individuals to identify those responsible and help bring them to justice.

"However unwilling victims may be initially to engage with police or other agencies, or to give evidence against the perpetrators, they will always be supported, listened to and protected from further harm.

"West Yorkshire Police, the West Yorkshire's Police and Crime Commissioner and partner agencies are committed to doing everything they possibly can to ensure that children are safe, cared for and protected from harm. We are committed to working closely with these partners and will take positive action against those who abuse or neglect children.

"I hope the outcomes of these trials will enable the victims to start the process of putting this trauma behind them and reassure any other potential victims that we will treat them with the utmost respect and sensitivity and take positive action against perpetrators."

A spokesman for the NSPCC said: "The immense bravery of the survivors in this case has ensured that four more members of this predatory gang have been brought to justice.

"These depraved men groomed, exploited and then repeatedly sexually abused vulnerable girls."

Home Secretary Sajid Javid added his opinion too: "These horrific crimes are sickening and, first and foremost, I commend the bravery of those who've suffered abuse in coming forward.

"I thank both the police and the Crown Prosecution Service for their dedication, and I am glad to see these offenders face justice.

"I've made a personal commitment to tackle child sexual abuse in all its forms and the significant investment we have provided to transform law enforcement's response is beginning to take effect.

"I am prepared to ask difficult questions about these types of offenders, and I will not stop until we have done everything possible to protect vulnerable children."

It seemed everyone was having their say. Everyone except me. I felt a prickle of annoyance at the police statement too:

However unwilling victims may be initially to engage with police or other agencies, or to give evidence against the perpetrators, they will always be supported, listened to and protected from further harm.

From my point of view, the police had not listened to me, supported me or protected me in all those years when I was preyed upon and abused. And they were equally as unwilling to engage with me as I was with them. The officers in the investigation had been brilliant. But before then, I felt the police had completely let me down. That part of the story seemed to have been conveniently whitewashed. So, when the ITV news contacted me, I decided to speak out; to give my side of the story.

"I'll do it," I agreed. "Anonymously, please."

Even though I knew the gang members were all in prison, I was still worried about recriminations, and I didn't want to give an interview at my home, or my parents' house, in case they recognised background wallpaper or furniture.

I was working at a children's nursery by now and so it was arranged that the film crew would interview us there. It was stomach-churning but absolutely fitting to bring the issue of grooming into the innocence of a children's nursery, alongside the sandpit and the wooden building blocks. These were the same children I wanted to protect.

We would be fully anonymised, and our voices would be changed. Even so, I was still very apprehensive. People around me kept insisting it was the right thing to do, and so I went along with it. I saw it as a step towards the future. I answered the questions, I followed the instructions, yet I felt like an imposter, thrust into someone else's life.

It seemed quite bizarre that I was to be the main headline on the evening news – on Dad's favourite programme. It could have been comical if it had not been so overwhelmingly poignant and sad. And even as I watched the interview back on TV the following night, I could not shake the conviction that I was in some way to blame for all of this. I hated the way that I felt, yet I could not change it. I didn't give any more interviews after that. Whatever I was hoping to gain from the process did not materialise, and perhaps it did not exist.

* * * *

The media interest inevitably died down and I tried to concentrate on my family and my work. I desperately wanted to shrug off my old life off like an ugly dress or an itchy jumper. To simply pull it over my head and throw it into the bin. Burn it even. To be done with it, once and for all.

But slowly, I began to realise that I could not simply flick a switch to change how I felt. It was a comfort to know that the men were in prison. But that did not change what had happened to me. I would have to find a way to live with it; somehow. I would never get over the abuse or move on from it. But I began to realise that I could instead make a space for it in my soul and carry it with me.

On the advice of my support workers, I instructed a solicitor and submitted an application for compensation through the Criminal Injuries Compensation Authority (CICA).

But their reply, which came a couple of months later, explained that I would not be eligible to claim compensation because of my own criminal record. The fact that I only had a criminal record because I was a victim of a grooming gang had completely escaped their notice. My criminal record was not a separate or unrelated issue. It was another aspect of the abuse.

"How can this be right?" I complained.

I was very short of money, not helped by my attendances at the three trials and my spells in hospital. Managing my unpredictable mental health was like carrying a bag of bricks on my back and it greatly affected my capacity to hold down a job. But my solicitor said there was little to be gained in appealing. As the CICA decision sunk in, the money became a secondary issue. I focused more on the belief that the abuse had to be my fault — that I had some part to play — and that was why CICA had refused my claim. They believed that I had some responsibility. And deep down, I did too. They reinforced my flawed conviction that I was to blame.

* * * *

In June 2019, I was doing a quick dash around the supermarket when a headline on the newsstand caught my eye.

"'We are truly sorry' say council after missed opportunities to stop grooming gang."

I stopped dead, all thoughts of my shopping list forgotten. I walked towards the newspapers as though I was walking into a burning building. It felt like self-sabotage to buy a copy, yet I had to. As I waited in the queue to pay, I felt as though everyone knew it was me, everyone knew I was Girl A. There was an accusatorial hum of conversation, which translated in my head as:

Should have gone to school instead of hanging round the bus station
If it was my daughter, I'd have kept her at home
Why did she keep on going back to them?

I knew it was all in my mind. I was the only one who laid the blame at my door. Yet that was more than I could cope with. Clutching the newspaper in my hand, and abandoning my shopping trolley, I dashed outside and found a bench. The headline related to the publication of a review into the Huddersfield grooming scandal. The independent report, by Dr Mark Peel, said that council staff were told by victims that they were being abused but no action was taken. Opportunities to save them, and other girls, were missed.

"Too bloody right," I muttered.

I read on that Dr Peel said details of young women caught in "the cycle of sexual exploitation" went undetected and unrecorded by skilled and experienced social workers and managers. This was despite one case file referring specifically to "sexual exploitation" by Asian males who gave one victim – known as 'Girl 8' – drugs and alcohol.

And after reviewing two case files, he wrote: "It is my contention that Children's Services officers knew at the time that these young women [were] most likely to have been engaged in inappropriate, exploitative and illegal sexual activity to the extent that they had sufficient evidence to conclude these vulnerable young women were at risk of 'serious harm'.

"In both instances however it would appear that, other than recording this information, no subsequent preventative safeguarding action was taken, and that thus an opportunity to break the child sexual exploitation (CSE) ring operating in Kirklees, and protect these girls directly and others more generally, was lost."

My eyes widened as I scanned further and saw that

Kirklees Council had apologised to girls that were "let down".

Chief Executive Jacqui Gedman said: "We absolutely agree with Dr Peel that a small number of the cases could, and should, have been handled differently at the time and on behalf of the council I want to apologise to the girls that we let down.

"This is a common theme in reviews of historic cases around the country and we must all ensure that we learn from the past.

"We now have a much greater understanding of the risks and issues involved in CSE and we can be confident that the progress of recent years would lead to very different actions today.

"We are actively encouraging people to come forward if they have any reason to think they have been abused.

"We know how difficult this can be, but our message is: we will listen to you, we will take action and we will learn from your experiences."

I gasped in annoyance.

"She has never apologised to me!" I exclaimed out loud. "Not once. That just isn't true."

Since the trial had ended, I'd had absolutely no contact from the council, from social services or the police or any other agencies. I was left completely on my own. Here was an article, published about the abuse which I had endured, and I didn't even know about it. I had no idea which girl I was – Girl 1, 2, 3, 4? I was just a number. Yet I didn't know which one.

The article continued to explain that Dr Peel, who was chair of Leeds Safeguarding Children Partnership, had worked only from social work case files. He did not review police or school files. He also did not interview any of the victims or staff of Kirklees Children's Services. He had, however, met with Kirklees councillors in private.

The newspaper explained that his independent review report did not conclusively describe and understand why young women known to Kirklees Council were not recognised as being subject to child sexual exploitation.

I certainly hadn't been interviewed. I wasn't even made aware a review was underway. Given the fact that we, the victims, had been ignored and let down right through all those years of abuse, it felt like a further slap in the face for us now to be excluded from the review also. Dr Peel had spoken to local councillors, but not to the victims.

A swell of bitterness rose in my gut. Possibly, probably, I would have refused to take part. But I would have liked to be offered the choice. That would have been the decent thing to do. For so long, I had been treated as an object, without emotions or feelings and without a mind of my own.

And this felt like a further twist of the knife.

Despite the concerns found in the case file extract for 'Girl 8' being reported by the victim's mother, her school, Kirklees Children's Services and at least one other local agency, no further action was taken to ensure her safety or identify the men in question.

Dr Peel wrote: "If remedial action had been taken in 2007 to safeguard her [and two other victims], links to others suffering exploitation might have been established, and the operation of the CSE ring discovered."

He said in two cases which included clear evidence of child sexual exploitation (CSE), crucial information had been completely omitted.

"It would appear that no action of any kind was taken in both these instances.

"No discussion with senior officers and managers, no checking of facts or communication with colleagues from other agencies and no direct engagement with the young people and their families in order to protect them."

And he argued that the lack of protective action suggested that sexual exploitation was seen as "nothing out of the ordinary or at least 'normal' for those young women".

This implied that some young women in need of help received a different and lower safeguarding standard of support.

He described "the seeming lack of concern and remedial action" as being "almost alien" in 2019 but that in 2007 it was common across the UK "both professionally and organisationally".

Dr Peel wrote: "It cannot be argued that Kirklees was simply unaware of the young women who latterly featured in the CSE court case."

He said the majority had open case files in their own right across or during the time period in question. He said evidence pointed to young women sporadically coming to the attention of social workers with a range of issues that, retrospectively, were due to sexual exploitation.

Yet this "fact" remained "undetected" and hence unrecorded to skilled and experienced workers and managers.

He said professional workers would have been unable to "piece together" sufficient evidence to point to CSE, a type of abuse he said was "largely unknown" more than a decade ago.

In a key section of the report, he wrote: "Unless the young women themselves had directly disclosed to social workers at the time that they were subject to a type of abuse we now recognise as sexually exploitative, or this had been raised by a third party, it is unlikely that social workers and their managers could have unilaterally come to such a conclusion, as they simply were (in the main) unaware of the issue, and consequently were not looking for it."

He continued: "It thus remains difficult for even the most skilled and experienced safeguarding professional to 'follow the breadcrumbs' linking individual young women to risk around CSE.

"In retrospect it is tempting to ask 'Why didn't they spot CSE when it was so obvious?' The simple fact here is that nobody spotted it, because we simply weren't looking."

Dr Peel suggested that there should be "a comprehensive review" of all target historic CSE case files held by Kirklees Children's Services beyond the 22 girls featured in the court case.

He added that his independent review should in no way be seen as an alternative to a public inquiry. He said the limiting four-month timeframe for the investigation meant he had to take a "least worst" approach.

But I was not hopeful of a public inquiry. I felt as though

the whole horrible episode had been hushed up and swept under the carpet. I didn't matter then, and I didn't matter now.

18

Grief and Hope

Throughout 2018, Dad had been complaining of niggly stomach cramps. Most of the time, he ignored them or brushed them off and only occasionally, when he was in real pain, would he let us know about them. He didn't like to make a fuss generally, and especially not about medical matters.

"I'm fine," he replied, whenever I tried to persuade him to make an appointment with the GP. "You know I'm not keen on doctors."

He was a typical bloke, in many ways. Dad's phobia of the medical profession, however, had a rational cause, for, when he was just a little boy, his mother was taken into hospital, and that was the last time he ever saw her. She had died from leukaemia, and, heartbreakingly, he was just nine years old. Dad was raised by a loving aunt, in Co Kerry, who then stepped in as a grandmother for me too and was a treasured member of our family. But the trauma of losing his mother at such a young age had left its mark on Dad.

So, as the stomach pains grew worse, he stubbornly refused to acknowledge them. It was only when he was doubled over in agony, one day, that Mum insisted on him seeing the GP. The surgery was a short walk from our family home, but Dad was in such discomfort that she had to drive him there. The GP sent him straight to hospital for urgent tests. By the time I got to hospital, after work that evening, he was already being warned to prepare himself for bad news.

"Don't worry, pet," he smiled, from his hospital bed. "I'm tough as old leather. You know that."

Even now, he was thinking of me, not himself. He didn't want me to worry. But the scans had found a cancerous tumour and Dad had surgery that same week to remove both the tumour and a section of his bowel. His surgeon hoped that the cancer was contained, and that he would need no further treatment. It was a big relief, and we were so thankful.

Even so, it was really hard for Dad, adjusting to a colostomy bag. He became very self-conscious. He was more vigilant too about his diet and for a while, he wouldn't go out for fear of having an accident with his bag. But it wasn't like him to be down for long and soon, he was adjusting to his new addition. He went back to work and he even started meeting up with his mates for a Guinness at St Pat's club. He made a good all-round recovery.

"Proud of you, Dad," I beamed.

But during lockdown in 2020, he started to feel unwell again and tests showed that his cancer had spread. On a video call with the hospital, his doctor announced they were unable to offer any more treatment.

"I'm really sorry," she said.

"Please," I begged. "Is there nothing at all you can do?

Can you at least see him in person before you make a final decision?"

She agreed to give Dad a face-to-face appointment and Mum and I were allowed to accompany him to hospital. At the end of the examination, the consultant said:

"I'm glad that I saw you. I do think you might benefit from chemotherapy."

We knew the situation was still very serious. But this was a small green shoot of hope, and we grasped it gratefully with both hands. Dad coped well with the chemo which followed; he drove himself to hospital for each session. He even took a packed lunch to pass the time.

We had been told the chemotherapy was not a cure. But there was no way I was prepared to just give up on him, and I researched his cancer online, night after night. We tried alternative remedies and a healthier diet. I couldn't imagine life without my dad and I was desperate to do everything I could. Besides, he had been there for me, through the years, when I was being abused. I remembered all those nights he had driven around in his trusty old truck, looking for me. I hadn't forgotten all the little DIY jobs he did for me, every time I rented a new place. Or the new furniture and carpets he bought for me. This was my way of saying thank you to him. It was my attempt to give Dad something back, in appreciation.

"You can count on me," I told him.

I was at my parents' house most days, running errands for him and taking him to appointments. Dad had been the one to pay for driving lessons for me, and he'd bought me my first car, the blue Micra, and my second too, a little silver Kia. I was pleased now to use my skills to help him out instead.

Then, Dad tripped down the stairs at home and broke his leg, and he needed even more support.

"I'll be your taxi driver," I offered. "No charge!"

In November 2021, I took Dad for an eye test, because he needed new glasses. As we walked into the optician's, and I glanced casually around the waiting room, I suddenly froze, petrified. There, staring right back at me, was Niaz Ahmed, known to me as Shaq.

"What's the matter?" Dad asked, taking a seat.

"There," I whispered. "It's Shaq. One of the gang."

Dad's face dropped and his whole body stiffened. Shaq was just a few years younger than my dad, and it must have been very hard for him to come face to face with the man, in a public place. But to Dad's credit, he muttered a little to himself and kept perfectly calm.

My whole body was trembling with shock. I wanted so much to show Shaq that I was no longer afraid and that he no longer ruled me. Yet I just couldn't pull it off. I was still so scared. Deep down, I was still 14 years old.

If a part of me hoped that Shaq might do the decent thing and leave, then I was fooling myself. He sat it out and stared right through me, his dark eyes boring a hole through the side of my head. I wanted so much to run away, but this was Dad's appointment, not mine, and I couldn't let him down.

Luckily, we were called in to see the optician a few minutes later and when we came out, Shaq was gone. But I felt unsettled and upset all day. I kept on checking my windows and doors, making sure I was safe. For the last few months, I had settled into something of a relaxed routine, believing all the men were behind bars. Now, I was back to looking over my shoulder. Back to living in fear. Later that week, I got a letter informing me that Shaq was being released from prison.

"Bit late for that now, when I've already seen him," I snapped.

In the weeks and months which followed, I got a letter telling me that Chiller had applied for open prison. There was another telling me that some of the gang members were being moved to an open prison and would be allowed out on escorted and unescorted home leave. The idea was terrifying. Not only did I risk bumping into them, but now they would have a reason to go after me. It was my testimony which had helped to put them all in jail. My only comfort was that Pretos, the ringleader, was in prison and would be for many years to come. But I was not foolish enough to think that I could escape his wrath. Even in jail, I knew he could orchestrate a wicked revenge on me, if he wished.

Once again, I thought about leaving Huddersfield, I dreamed of fleeing to the other side of the country, even to the other side of the world.

Yet it was not so simple. I wanted to be near my family, especially Dad, because his health was poor. He needed me and I could not let him down. My children were settled in the neighbourhood. I had a job and a home here. And besides, I wondered why I should be the one to move. I was supposed to be the victim in all of this. I had to keep reminding myself of that.

One day, as I walked to the shops, I spotted Bully coming up the street towards me. In my daydreams, I had imagined myself coming face to face with the gang members so many times. I had hoped I would look them in the eye and march past them with dignity. Perhaps I would even share a few choice words. Above all, I would not be afraid.

But in the cold harsh reality of the street, just as in the optician's, my courage deserted me. I turned and ran, back up the street, fumbling my keys out of my pocket. I slammed the front door behind me and sank to the carpet, with my blood sloshing and pounding in my ears.

"You're safe," I told myself. "You're safe. You're fine now."

But as the tears flowed, I realised how hollow and meaningless my platitudes were. Would I ever really be safe? It was a question I often asked myself but was never able to answer.

Dad's broken leg did not heal and, over Christmas 2021, he was admitted once again to hospital. His condition deteriorated and we were warned his cancer was spreading and he was terminally ill. I spent every day with him, knowing that our time was running out. He died peacefully in hospital on March 19, 2022, aged 75.

I was broken-hearted. I had suffered so much through my teenage years, but nothing compared to the loss of my dear dad. Right up to his dying breath, I had hoped against hope that he might pull through. I always was a daddy's girl and always will be. That will never change. Right through the dark days of the grooming gang, he was the one who anchored me and brought me home, each time I feared I might be swept out into rough seas.

One day, I will see him again for another big hug. Sometimes, as I'm walking down the main road, I hear a grumbly engine in the distance and I know that it's Dad in his truck, looking out for me and making sure that I get home safely.

* * * *

In 2023, I am still in the same two-bedroom house in Huddersfield, still in the place where my life fell apart. It's my hope that, one day, I will put it all back together and the pieces will slot in again as they once did. I am working in the hospitality industry, training as a chef, and enjoying the long and demanding shifts. My criminal record makes it tough for me to get work, but I don't give up easily. I am determined to be a success in a career that lets me make a difference.

My son is currently living away from the family home, but I see him as much as I can. I accept fully I haven't been the best Mum in the past, but it is my life's goal to be a better parent and a better person. Who knows, one day I might flourish in spite of, or because of, what happened to me as a child. I may be able to make past trauma work in my favour.

I can't change the path I took, rather I was forced to take, aged 14. But I can speak out to try and make sure that my child – and all children – grow up knowing about the evils of grooming. We have to talk about child sexual exploitation and educate our children, in order to cleanse society of this evil. It is unpalatable and uncomfortable. But hiding from it just helps it to fester and thrive underground. It's my aim to bring grooming into the daily vocabulary and consciousness so parents and police can spot the signs and act before their children are swallowed up, as I was.

Operation Tendersea continues, there was yet another trial in 2020, bringing the number of trials to six, and many more convictions along the way. Sadly, many more victims too. By 2020, there were 35 men convicted, serving a total sentence of 377 and a half years.

In April this year, the government announced new measures to tackle grooming gangs and claimed that political correctness would not stand in the way of cracking down on the perpetrators. A new grooming gang task force will be set up with specialist officers, supported by the National Crime Agency, helping local forces and offering the use of ethnicity data to assist police investigations.

Home Secretary Suella Braverman said: "The time has come to make right one of the greatest injustices seen in Britain in modern times. The systematic rape, exploitation and abuse of young girls by organised gangs of older men – and the disgraceful failure of the authorities to act despite ample evidence – is a stain on our country."

The Prime Minister Rishi Sunak warned that for too long "political correctness has stopped us from weeding out vile criminals who prey on children and young women".

Even now, after three trials and all those convictions, I still don't feel as though I've been absolved of responsibility. I would welcome help and support from the agencies who failed me the first time around. I would like them to recognise that I am the victim in this.

We will never rid the world of paedophiles. There will always be grooming gangs, and there will always be people who want to exploit and brainwash children. In addition to these new government ideas, we need to educate girls to speak out and to believe in themselves. And we need to support them when they do.

If I could rewind back to 2005, to the girl who ran across the school fields, her hair flying in the wind as she played truant, I would urge her to speak out. I would urge her to scream at the top of her voice about the men she met at the bus station, who gave her vodka and cigarettes and hooked her hair behind her ear.

I was let down by the police, the social services, and, I will always believe, by myself. But most of all, by the men who abused and raped me on an almost daily basis for over four years.

I would like to tell every child that your most powerful weapon is your voice, and you must use it always.

Other bestselling Mirror Books

The Asylum
Carol Minto
With Ann and Joe Cusack

Born into poverty and with mostly absent parents, Carol helped to raise her nine siblings. But when she was just 11 years old, her older brother began to sexually abuse her.

After four years, Carol managed to escape – and ran away from home. Picked up by social services they placed her at the infamous Aston Hall psychiatric hospital in Derby where she was stripped, sedated, assaulted and raped by the doctor in charge.

This is the full story of how she overcame unimaginable suffering, to find the solace she has today as a mother and grandmother.

MIRROR BOOKS

written by Ann and Joe Cusack

The Boy With
A Pound In His Pocket
Jade Akoum

With Ann and Joe Cusack

**Yousef Makki was stabbed in the heart by one
of his friends on a quiet, leafy street in the wealthy
Manchester suburb of Hale Barns.**

Just four months after he was killed, a jury found his friend not
guilty of murder or manslaughter. Yousef died from a single stab
wound to the chest.

When his sister, Jade, collected his blood-stained clothes, he had
a single pound coin in his pocket. This is Jade's moving, personal
story of how the fight for justice has transformed her life.

MIRROR BOOKS

Other bestselling Mirror Books

A Mother's Job
Joy Dove

With Ann and Joe Cusack

**While Jodey Whiting was stuck in hospital
battling pneumonia over Christmas, a letter
dropped on her doormat from the Department for Work
and Pensions, asking her to attend an assessment.
It was a letter she never saw...**

Despite suffering from major health problems and needing daily care, the powers-that-be callously halted benefit payments for the mum-of-nine. While waiting for her appeal, and with no money coming in, Jodey killed herself, aged just 42. This is the story of her mother Joy's brave and inspirational fight for justice.

written by Ann and Joe Cusack

Abandoned
Monica Allan

With Ann and Joe Cusack

Monica was just five years old when her mother tried to kill her by forcing her head under running bathroom taps. She had already tried to strangle her as a baby.

Escaping into foster care, Monica would go on to experience horrific physical and sexual abuse. She tried to find a new life and raise a loving family of her own. But living with the devastating secrets that had been buried for so long proved too painful.

Enough was enough. To live again, she knew she had to confront the demons of her past.

MIRROR BOOKS